# Let Us Pray

R. C. Sproul
John MacArthur
John Piper
Joel Beeke
Steven Lawson
W. Robert Godfrey
Richard D. Phillips
Hywel Jones
Michael Haykin
Phil Johnson
Bruce Bickel

Don Kistler, General Editor

The Northampton Press
. . .for instruction in righteousness. . .

The Northampton Press
A Division of Don Kistler Ministries, Inc.
P.O. Box 781135, Orlando, FL 32878-1135
www.northamptonpress.org

*

ISBN 978-0-9847062-0-4

*

*

The publishing of this book has been made possible through the generosity of Christ the Redeemer Reformed Presbyterian Church of Eureka, CA. The publisher wishes to acknowledge their kindness in making this book available.

*

Library of Congress Cataloging-in-publication Data

Let us pray / R.C. Sproul ... [et al.] ; Don Kistler, general editor.
    p. cm.
ISBN 978-0-9847062-0-4 (alk. paper)
1. Prayer--Christianity. I. Sproul, R. C. (Robert Charles), 1939- II. Kistler, Don.
  BV210.3.L47 2011
  248.3'2--dc23
                                        2011041726

# Contents

# Author Bios

(The authors are listed in the order in which they appear in the book.)

**Dr. R.C. Sproul** is the founder and president of Ligonier Ministries, and is the president of the Ligonier Academy. He is also the preaching pastor at St. Andrew's Chapel in Sanford, FL, and is the author of more than 80 books.

**Dr. John MacArthur** has been the pastor/teacher of Grace Community Church in Southern California for 40 years. He also serves as President of the Master's College and Seminary. He has authored over 400 books and study guides.

**Dr. John Piper** has been the pastor of Bethlehem Baptist Church in Minneapolis, MN for over 30 years. He is the author of more than 30 books.

**Dr. Joel Beeke** is the founder and president of Puritan Reformed Theological Seminary in Grand Rapids, MI. He serves as Professor of Systematic Theology and Homiletics. He is also pastor of Heritage Netherlands Reformed Congregation in Grand Rapids. He has written, co-authored, or edited 70 books.

**Dr. Steven J. Lawson** is senior pastor of Christ Fellowship Baptist Church in Mobile, AL. He is the author of 16 books and has pastored for over 30 years.

**Dr. W. Robert Godfrey** is the president of Westminster Seminary California. He is a council member of the Alliance of Confessing Evangelicals.

**Richard D. Phillips** is the pastor of Second Presbyterian Church, Greenville, SC. He chairs the Philadelphia Conference on Reformed Theology, founded by the late James Boice. He is the author of 21 books.

**Dr. Hywel R. Jones** has been Professor of Practical Theology at Westminster Seminary California since 2000. Prior to that he was Editorial Director of the Banner of Truth Trust for four years and Lecturer at London Theological Seminary since its inception in 1977, becoming its first Principal in 1985. He was ordained in 1963 in the Presbyterian Church of Wales and served in several pastorates. He and his wife, Nansi, have been married for 50 years and have three adult children and six grandchildren. He is the author of several books. The most recent are commmentaries on Hebrews, Job, Psalm 119 and Philippians.

**Dr. Michael A. G. Haykin** serves as the Professor of Church History and Biblical Spirituality at the Southern Baptist Theological Seminary in Louisville, KY. He has authored 10 books.

**Phil Johnson** is the Executive Director of Grace to You. He has been closely associated with John MacArthur since 1981 and edits most of John's major books. But he may be best known for several popular websites he maintains, including The Spurgeon Archive and The Hall of Church History. Phil has a bachelor's degree in theology from Moody Bible Institute (class of 1975) and was an editor at Moody Press before coming to Grace Community Church. He is an elder at Grace Community Church and pastors the GraceLife fellowship group.

**Dr. Bruce Bickel** is the president and founder of Transformational Leadership Group. He is the author of *Light and Heat: The Puritan View of the Pulpit.*

**Dr. Don Kistler** was the founder of Soli Deo Gloria Publications, and is the founder and president of The Northampton Press. He has written two books and has edited more than 400 books, most of those first-time reprints of Puritan writings.

# Foreword
## Don Kistler

Yet another book on prayer? Yes, in spite of the innumerable books on the subject out there, it seems that we've not learned much about prayer. But perhaps this book has a distinction. It's not a "how to" book on prayer. It's not a "if you will do this, then God will do that" book on prayer. It's not a "how to get what you want out of God" book on prayer. And it is not a "here's a formula for prayer" book.

This book had its genesis in my own experiences with praying people. I noticed some time ago that, for most of the folks with whom I prayed, prayer was really little more than a litany of petitions, almost a shopping list of all the things God would need to do to ensure that they had a good day. This was often a list of body parts that needed to be healed, either on the one doing the praying or someone close to them.

If not that, then it was a newscast, letting God in on all the things going on in His universe that evidently were escaping His notice. I remember some years ago sitting in a Sunday evening worship service where, when asked to pray, a certain elder said this, "Lord, you may not know it, but Mrs. _____ is in the hospital." I couldn't help but think to myself, "Why bother praying to a God who may or may not know that already?"

Having said that, I grant that it is absolutely true that the Lord Jesus tells us to make our requests known to Him. That is undeniable. Petitions are a part of prayer, but petitions are not the totality of all that prayer is.

I've heard various preachers describe prayer as "a conversation with God," but I've not heard them address the part about letting God speak (not audibly, of course). Isn't conversation a two-way thing? What kind of a conversation is it if one person does all the talking?

What this compilation of essays by various authors attempts to do is to show that prayer is to be God-centered and God-focused as well as God-directed. One needs only look at the prayers of our Lord, as well as those of the Apostle Paul, to see that they began with God and ended with God. Praise was first and foremost in their minds. Addressing God with reverence and awe was the norm.

Each author has used his Bible version of choice. These are the King James Version (KJV), the New King James Version (NKJV), the New American Standard Bible (NASB), the New International Version (NIV), and the English Standard Version (ESV).

The authors here did not consult each other beforehand, so there will be some inevitable overlap in what they say. But their salient points are worthy to be repeated.

How interesting that when the disciples approached their Lord regarding prayer, they did not say, "Teach us HOW to pray," but rather, "Teach us TO pray." May it please the Lord to use this book to teach us to pray, to pray biblically, and to pray in a manner that is worthy of God. May our primary concern be the same as that of our Lord, to hallow His name.

# Why Pray?

## R. C. Sproul

(This material is taken from *Does Prayer Change Things?* © 2009 by Reformation Trust Publishing, and is used with permission of the publisher.)

Nothing escapes God's notice; nothing oversteps the boundaries of His power. God is authoritative in all things. If I thought even for one moment that a single molecule were running loose in the universe outside the control and domain of almighty God, I wouldn't sleep tonight. My confidence in the future rests in my confidence in the God who controls history. But how does God exercise that control and manifest that authority? How does God bring to pass the things He has sovereignly decreed?

Augustine said that nothing happens in this universe apart from the will of God and that, in a certain sense, God ordains everything that happens. Augustine was not attempting to absolve men of responsibility for their actions, but his teaching raises a question: If God is sovereign over the actions and intents of men, why pray at all? A secondary concern revolves around the question, "Does prayer really change anything?"

Let me answer the first question by stating that the sovereign God commands by His sovereign, holy Word that we pray. Prayer is not optional for the Christian; it is required.

We might ask, "What if it doesn't do anything?" That is not the issue. Regardless of whether prayer does any good, if God commands us to pray, we must pray. It is reason enough that the Lord God of the universe, the Creator and Sustainer of all things, commands it. Yet He not only commands us to pray, but also invites us to make our requests known. James says that we

do not have because we do not ask (James 4:2). He also tells us
that the prayer of a righteous man accomplishes much (James
5:16). Time and again the Bible says that prayer is an effective
tool. It is useful; it works.

John Calvin, in the *Institutes of the Christian Religion*, makes
some profound observations regarding prayer:

> But, someone will say, does God not know, even without
> being reminded, both in what respect we are troubled and
> what is expedient for us, so that it may seem in a sense su-
> perfluous that he should be stirred up by our prayers—as if
> he were drowsily blinking or even sleeping until he is
> aroused by our voices? But they who thus reason do not
> observe to what end the Lord instructed his people to pray,
> for he ordained it not so much for his own sake as for
> ours. Now he wills—as is right—that his due be rendered to
> him, in the recognition that everything men desire and ac-
> count conducive to their own profit comes from him, and
> in the attestation of this by prayers. But the profit of this
> sacrifice also, by which he is worshiped, returns to us. Ac-
> cordingly, the holy fathers, the more confidently they ex-
> tolled God's benefits among themselves and others, were
> the more keenly aroused pray . . . .
>
> Still it is very important for us to call upon him: First,
> that our hearts may be fired with a zealous and burning
> desire ever to seek, love, and serve him, while we become
> accustomed in every need to flee to him as to a sacred an-
> chor. Secondly, that there may enter our hearts no desire
> and no wish at all of which we should be ashamed to make
> him a witness, while we learn to set all our wishes before
> his eyes, and even to pour out our whole hearts. Thirdly,
> that we be prepared to receive his benefits with true grati-
> tude of heart and thanksgiving, benefits that our prayer
> reminds us come from his hand. (Calvin, *Institutes of the
> Christian Religion*, trans. Ford Lewis Battles, ed. John T.
> McNeill [Louisville: Westminster John Knox, 1960], Book
> 3, chapter 20, section 3.)

Prayer, like everything else in the Christian life, is for God's glory and for our benefit, in that order. Everything that God does, everything that God allows and ordains, is, in the supreme sense, for His glory. It is also true that while God seeks His own glory supremely, man benefits when God is glorified. We pray to glorify God, but we also pray in order to receive the benefits of prayer from His hand. Prayer is for our benefit, even in light of the fact that God knows the end from the beginning. It is our privilege to bring the whole of our finite existence into the glory of His infinite presence.

## A Discourse with God

One of the great themes of the Reformation was the idea that all of life is to be lived under the authority of God, to the glory of God, in the presence of God. Prayer is not simply soliloquy, a mere exercise in therapeutic self-analysis, or a religious recitation. Prayer is discourse with the personal God Himself. There, in the act and dynamic of praying, I bring my whole life under His gaze. Yes, He knows what is in my mind, but I still have the privilege of articulating to Him what is there. He says: "Come. Speak to Me. Make your requests known to Me." So we come in order to know Him and to be known by Him.

There is something erroneous in the question, "If God knows everything, why pray?" The question assumes that prayer is one-dimensional and is defined simply as supplication or intercession. On the contrary, prayer is multidimensional. God's sovereignty casts no shadow over the prayer of adoration. God's foreknowledge or determinate counsel does not negate the prayer of praise. The only thing it should do is give us greater reason for expressing our adoration for who God is. If God knows what I'm going to say before I say it, His knowledge, rather than limiting my prayer, enhances the beauty of my praise.

My wife and I are as close as two people can be. Often I know what she's going to say almost before she says it. The reverse is also true. But I still like to hear her say what is on her mind. If that is true of man, how much more true is it of God? We have the matchless privilege of sharing our innermost thoughts with God. Of course, we could simply enter our prayer closets, let God read our minds, and call that prayer. But that's not communion, and it's certainly not communication.

We are creatures who communicate primarily through speech. Spoken prayer is obviously a form of speech, a way for us to commune and communicate with God. There is a certain sense in which God's sovereignty should influence our attitude toward prayer, at least with respect to adoration. If anything, our understanding of God's sovereignty should provoke us to an intense prayer life of thanksgiving. Because of such knowledge, we should see that every benefit, every good and perfect gift, is an expression of the abundance of His grace. The more we understand God's sovereignty, the more our prayers will be filled with thanksgiving.

In what way does God's sovereignty negatively affect the prayer of contrition, of confession? Perhaps we could draw the conclusion that our sin is ultimately God's responsibility, and that our confession is an accusation of guilt against God Himself. Every true Christian knows that he cannot blame God for his sin. I may not understand the relationship between divine sovereignty and human responsibility, but I do realize that what stems from the wickedness of my own heart may not be assigned to the will of God. So we must pray because we are guilty, pleading the pardon of the Holy One whom we have offended.

## Does Prayer Change Anything?

But what about intercession and supplication? It's nice to talk about the religious, spiritual, and psychological benefits (and whatever else might derive from prayer), but what about the real question—Does prayer make any difference? Does it really change anything? Someone once asked me that question, only in a slightly different manner: "Does prayer change God's mind?" My answer brought storms of protest. I said simply, "No." Now, if the person had asked me, "Does prayer change *things*?" I would have answered, "Of course!"

The Bible says there are certain things that God has decreed from all eternity. Those things will inevitably come to pass. If you were to pray individually, or if you and I were to join forces in prayer, or if all the Christians of the world were to pray collectively, it would not change what God, in His hidden counsel, has determined to do. If we decided to pray for Jesus not to return, He still would return. You might ask, though, "Doesn't the Bible say that if two or three agree on anything, they'll get it?" Yes, it does, but that passage is talking about church discipline, not prayer requests. So we must take all the biblical teaching on prayer into account and not isolate one passage from the rest. We must approach the matter in light of the whole of Scripture, resisting an atomistic reading.

Again, you might ask, "Doesn't the Bible say from time to time that God repents?" Yes, the Old Testament certainly says so. The book of Jonah tells us that God "repented of" the judgment He had planned for the people of Nineveh (Jonah 3:10, KJV). In using the concept of repentance here, the Bible is describing God, who is Spirit, in what theologians call "anthropomorphic" language. Obviously the Bible does not mean that God repented in the way we would repent; otherwise, we could rightly assume that God had sinned and therefore would need a savior Himself. What it clearly means is that God removed the threat of judgment from the people. The Hebrew word *nacham*, translated "repent" in the King James Version, means "comforted" or "eased" in this case. God was comforted and felt at ease that the people had turned from their sin, and therefore He revoked the sentence of judgment He had imposed.

When God hangs His sword of judgment over people's heads, and they repent and He then withholds His judgment, has He really changed His mind, like a chameleon?

The mind of God does not change; God is not a thing. *Things* change, and they change according to His sovereign will, which He exercises through secondary means and secondary activities. The prayer of His people is one of the means He uses to bring things to pass in this world. So if you ask me whether prayer changes things, I answer with an unhesitating "Yes!"

It is impossible to know how much of human history reflects God's immediate intervention and how much reveals God working through human agents. Calvin's favorite example of this was the book of Job. The Sabeans and the Chaldeans had taken Job's donkeys and camels. Why? Because Satan had stirred their hearts to do so. But why? Because Satan had received permission from God to test Job's faithfulness in any way he so desired, short of taking Job's life. Why had God agreed to such a thing? For three reasons: (1) to silence the slander of Satan; (2) to vindicate Himself; and (3) to vindicate Job from the slander of Satan. All of these reasons are perfectly righteous justifications for God's actions.

By contrast, Satan's purpose in stirring up these two groups was to cause Job to blaspheme God—an altogether wicked motive. But we notice that Satan did not do something supernatural to accomplish his ends. He chose human agents—the Sabeans and Chaldeans, who were evil by nature—to steal Job's animals.

The Sabeans and Chaldeans were known for their thievery and murderous way of life. Their will was involved, but there was no coercion. God's purpose was accomplished through their wicked actions.

The Sabeans and Chaldeans were free to choose, but for them, as for us, freedom always means freedom within limits. We must not, however, confuse human freedom and human autonomy. There will always be a conflict between divine sovereignty and human autonomy. There is never a conflict between divine sovereignty and human freedom. The Bible says that man is free, but he is not an autonomous law unto himself.

Suppose the Sabeans and Chaldeans had prayed, "Lead us not into temptation, but deliver us from the evil one." I'm absolutely certain that Job's animals still would have been stolen. But I'm equally certain that the Sabeans and Chaldeans would not have been responsible because their prayer would have altered the entire situation. There is freedom within limits, and within those limits our prayers can change things. The Scriptures tell us that Elijah, through prayer, was given power to command the rain. He was not dissuaded from praying by his understanding of divine sovereignty.

### The Prayers of the Son of God

No human being has ever had a more profound understanding of divine sovereignty than Jesus. No man ever prayed more fiercely or more effectively. Even in Gethsemane, He requested an option, a different way. When the request was denied, He bowed to the Father's will. The very reason we pray is because of God's sovereignty, because we believe that God has it within His power to order things according to His purpose. That is what sovereignty is all about—ordering things according to God's purpose. So, then, does prayer change God's mind? No! Does prayer change things? Yes, of course!

The promise of the Scriptures is that "The prayer of a righteous person has great power as it is working" (James 5:16). The problem is that we are not all that righteous. What prayer most often changes is the wickedness and the hardness of our own hearts. That alone would be reason enough to pray, even if none of the other reasons were valid or true.

In a sermon titled "The Most High, a Prayer-Hearing God," Jonathan Edwards gave two reasons why God requires prayer:

> With respect to God, prayer is but a sensible acknowledgement of our dependence on him to his glory. As he hath made all things for his own glory, so he will be glorified and acknowledged by his creatures; and it is fit that he should require this of those who would be subjects of his mercy . . . it is a suitable acknowledgement of our dependence on the power and mercy of God for that which we need, and but a suitable honor paid to the great Author and Fountain of all good.
>
> With respect to ourselves, God requires prayer of us . . . Fervent prayer in many ways tends to prepare the heart. Hereby is excited a sense of our need. . .whereby the mind is more prepared to prize the mercy we seek. Our prayer to God may excite in us a suitable sense and consideration of our dependence on God for the mercy we ask, and a suitable exercise of faith in God's sufficiency, so that we may be prepared to glorify his name when the mercy is received. (*The Works of Jonathan Edwards* [Carlisle, Pa.: Banner of Truth Trust, 1974], 116)

All that God does is for His glory first and for our benefit second. We pray because God commands us to pray, because it glorifies Him, and because it benefits us.

# Prayer as Worship
## John MacArthur

"Pray then like this: "Our Father in heaven, hallowed be your name. Your kingdom come, your will be done, on earth as it is in heaven. Give us this day our daily bread, and forgive us our debts, as we also have forgiven our debtors. And lead us not into temptation, but deliver us from evil." Matthew 6:9–13 (NASB)

Study the exemplary prayers in Scripture and you cannot help noticing that all of them are brief and simple. Prayer that is heartfelt, urgent, and unfeigned *must* be of that style. Verbiage and windbaggery are badges of insincerity, especially in prayer. The prayer of the publican in Luke 18:13 is as short and to the point as possible: "God, be merciful to me, a sinner!" Then there's the prayer of the thief on the cross: "Jesus, remember me when You come in Your kingdom!" (Luke 23:42). Those prayers are cut from the same cloth as Peter's cry for help when he was walking on water—sometimes cited as the shortest prayer in the Bible: "Lord, save me" (Matthew 14:30).

Scripture records very few long prayers. Much of Psalm 119 is addressed to God in the language of prayer, and, of course, that is the Bible's longest chapter. Other than that, Nehemiah 9:5–38 contains the longest prayer in all of Scripture, and it can be read aloud with expression in less than seven minutes. John 17 is the New Testament's longest prayer. It's also the longest of Jesus' recorded prayers, just twenty-six verses long.

We know, of course, that Jesus prayed much longer prayers than that because Scripture records several instances where He prayed in solitude for extended periods of time (Matthew 14:23; Mark 6:46). When it suited Him, He would even spend the entire night in prayer (Luke 6:12). It was His habit thus to pray, both privately and with His disciples (John 18:2). And the pattern was clear: His long prayers were the ones He prayed in private. His public prayers were perfect examples of crisp, forthright plain-speaking.

Listening to Jesus pray and observing His constant dependence on private prayer gave the disciples an appetite for prayer. So they asked Him, "Lord, teach us to pray" (Luke 11:1). He responded by repeating the very same model prayer He gave in the Sermon on the Mount. We call it "The Lord's Prayer." We ought rather to think of it as "The Disciples' Prayer," because its centerpiece is a petition for divine forgiveness, something Jesus would never need to pray for. Like all great praying, it is both succinct and unpretentious. There is not a wasted word, not a hint of vain repetition, and not a single note of ostentation or ceremony in the whole prayer:

> And He said to them, "When you pray, say: 'Father, hallowed be Your name. Your kingdom come. Give us each day our daily bread. And forgive us our sins, For we ourselves also forgive everyone who is indebted to us. And lead us not into temptation'" (Luke 11:2-4).

That prayer was a pattern for the disciples to follow, not a mantra to be recited without engaging the mind or passions. The various elements of Jesus' prayer are all reminders of what our praying ought to include: praise, petition, penitence, and a plea for grace in our sanctification. Those are not only the key elements of prayer, they are also some of the principal features of authentic worship. The parallelism between prayer and worship is no coincidence. Prayer is the distilled essence of worship.

That perspective is often lost in this era of self-focused, subjective, felt-needs-oriented religion. Multitudes think of prayer as nothing more than a way to get whatever they want from God. Prayer is reduced to a superstitious means of gain—and some will tell you that God is obligated to deliver the goods. Religious television is full of charlatans who insist that God *must* grant whatever you ask for *if* you can muster enough "faith" and refuse to entertain any "doubt." *Faith* in their lexicon is a kind of blind credulity, usually bolstered by some kind of "positive confession." *Doubt,* as they might describe it, is any rational or biblical qualm about whether the thing you desire is in accord with the will of God. Those, of course, are not biblical definitions of faith and doubt. Nor can anyone's prayer legitimately be called a "prayer offered in faith" (James 5:15) if it is contrary to the will of God.

Charismatics are not the only ones who see prayer as nothing more than a kind of utilitarian wish list. Plenty of mainstream evangelicals and old-style fundamentalists seem confused about the purpose of prayer, too. John R. Rice, an influential fundamentalist pastor, wrote a bestselling book in 1942 titled *Prayer—Asking and Receiving.* He wrote, "Prayer is not praise, adoration, meditation, humiliation nor confession, but *asking.* . . . Praise is not prayer, and prayer is not praise. Prayer is asking. . . . Adoration is not prayer, and prayer is not adoration. Prayer is always *asking.* It is not anything else but asking."[1]

There are several problems with that perspective. First, Jesus' model prayer is more than merely "asking." It does include that; there are petitions for daily bread (the barest of material needs) and forgiveness (the most urgent of spiritual needs). But the

---

1. John R. Rice, *Prayer—Asking and Receiving* (Muphreesboro, TN: Sword of the Lord, 1942), 29.

model prayer Jesus gave His disciples also includes at least four
of the five elements Dr. Rice wanted to eliminate from his
definition of prayer: praise, adoration, humiliation, and
confession.

Remove praise and penitence from the Lord's Prayer and
you have gutted it. Insist that proper prayer "is not anything else
but asking," and you overthrow one of the central lessons we
learn from Jesus' example, that prayer is first and foremost an
act of *worship*. Even worse, such teaching sets up a kind of role
reversal between the one praying and the God to whom he
prays.

The Bible teaches that God is sovereign and that we are His
slaves. "Name-it-and-claim-it" theology teaches that man is
sovereign and God is his servant. The person praying thinks he
is in the demand-and-command position, with God in the role
of the servant who is obligated to cough up whatever we ask for.
As I've pointed out elsewhere,[2] that has more in common with
pagan cargo cults than with biblical Christianity.

Prayer is much more than merely asking and receiving. It is
indeed a great privilege to come boldly before the throne of
grace and to let our requests be made known to God (Hebrews
4:16; Philippians 4:6). Scripture repeatedly promises that if we
ask for anything in faith, God *will* answer—meaning if we ask in
accord with God's will as prompted by His Spirit, He will always
graciously and generously respond (Matthew 7:7-11; 17:20;
21:22; Mark 11:24; James 1:6; 1 John 3:22). He often grants our
requests "exceeding abundantly above all that we ask or think"
(Ephesians 3:20, KJV).

---

[2] John MacArthur, *Charismatic Chaos* (Grand Rapids: Zondervan, 1992), 264-
90.

But the nature of a truly *faithful* prayer is clearly spelled out in 1 John 5:14: "This is the confidence which we have before Him, that, if we ask anything *according to His will*, He hears us" (emphasis added). In other words, the promise of answered prayer is not an unqualified blank check. The promise is made only to faithful, obedient, sober-minded, biblically-informed Christians whose prayers are in harmony with the will of God. It's not a guarantee of cargo to every gullible or superstitious religious enthusiast who uses Jesus' name as if it were an abracadabra. Jesus said, *"If you abide in Me, and My words abide in you*, ask whatever you wish, and it will be done for you" (John 15:7, emphasis added).

That's because far from being merely a wish list, godly prayer is fundamentally an act of *worship*. It is an expression of our praise, our unworthiness, our desire to see God's will fulfilled, and our utter dependence on Him for all our needs. Thus every aspect of prayer is an act of worship. That includes the petitions we make, because when we properly make our requests known to God—without anxiety, through prayer and supplication, and with thanksgiving (Philippians 4:6)—we are acknowledging His sovereignty, confessing our own total reliance on His grace and power, and looking to Him as Lord and Provider and Ruler of the universe—not as some kind of celestial Santa. Proper prayer is pure worship, even when we are making requests.

The God-ward focus of Jesus' model prayer is impossible to miss. The prayer starts with praise of God's name. It expresses a willingness for His Kingdom to come and His will to be done. Pure worship thus precedes and sets the context for supplication. Those opening lines establish the focal point of the prayer: *the glory of God and His Kingdom*. In other words, the supplicant is concerned first of all not for his personal wish list, but for the honor of God and the extension of His Kingdom.

Everything else fits into that context, so that the whole agenda of the prayer is determined by the Kingdom and glory of God. That is perhaps the most important perspective to keep in mind in all our praying.

Jesus said, "Whatever you ask in My name, that will I do, so that the Father may be glorified in the Son" (John 14:13). The purpose of all legitimate prayer is not to fulfill the felt-needs or material desires of the one praying, but to acknowledge the sovereignty of God and to magnify His glory. Prayer is not about getting what I want, but about the fulfillment of God's will. The proper objective of prayer is not to enlarge my borders, build my empire, or expand my wallet but to further the Kingdom of God. The point is not to elevate my name but to hallow God's name. Everything in prayer revolves around who God is, what God wants, and how God is to be glorified. That is the sum and substance of proper praying.

Any prayers that are self-consuming, self-indulgent, self-aggrandizing; any prayers that seek whatever I want no matter what God wants; any prayers that suggest God *must* deliver because I have demanded it—those are prayers that take His name in vain. Such praying is an egregious sin against the nature of God, against the will of God, and against the Word of God.

"Name it, claim it" prayers; the notion that God wants you always healthy, wealthy, prosperous, and successful; and lists of selfish requests are all quite at odds with the spirit of Jesus' model prayer. Such requests are expressly excluded from the many promises that God will hear and answer our prayers (James 4:3). The faulty belief that underlies all such praying is no small error. It is rooted in a serious misunderstanding about the nature of God.

Because prayer is an act of worship, to offer a prayer based on such a heinous perversion of God's character is tantamount to worshiping a false god. To put it bluntly, when someone presents God with a wish list rooted in greed, materialism, or other expressions of pure self-interest, then demands that God deliver the goods as if He were a genie, that is no prayer at all. It is an act of blasphemy. It is as abominable as the crassest form of pagan worship.

The prayers of godly people in Scripture were nothing like that. Consider the prayers of three prophets who were in truly dire situations. Jeremiah, for example, was in prison. He had preached to a nation of people who would not hear. They just wanted to shut his mouth. They were not interested in anything he or his God had to say. Ultimately they threw him in a pit. He had seen no measurable "success" in his ministry (as the world counts success). Jeremiah 32:16-23 records his prayer:

> I prayed to the LORD, saying, "Ah Lord GOD! Behold, You have made the heavens and the earth by Your great power and by Your outstretched arm! Nothing is too difficult for You, who shows lovingkindness to thousands, but repays the iniquity of fathers into the bosom of their children after them, O great and mighty God. The LORD of hosts is His name; great in counsel and mighty in deed, whose eyes are open to all the ways of the sons of men, giving to everyone according to his ways and according to the fruit of his deeds; who has set signs and wonders in the land of Egypt, *and* even to this day both in Israel and among mankind; and You have made a name for Yourself, as at this day.
>
> "You brought Your people Israel out of the land of Egypt with signs and with wonders, and with a strong hand and with an outstretched arm and with great terror; and gave them this land, which You swore to their forefathers to give them, a land flowing with milk and honey.

"They came in and took possession of it, but they did
not obey Your voice or walk in Your law; they have done
nothing of all that You commanded them to do; therefore
You have made all this calamity come upon them."

Here is a man in great distress, torn with feelings of loneli-
ness and grief, despairing of hope for his people, rejected by the
entire nation. But the preoccupation of his heart was to extol
the glory, the majesty, the name, the honor, and the works of
God. He was not preoccupied with his own pain. He was not
obsessed with being liberated from his circumstances. Out of his
suffering came worship.

All our prayers should be of that flavor.

Daniel, caught in the transition between two great world
empires, was interceding on behalf of a dispossessed people in a
foreign land. But notice the spirit with which he brought his
requests. He tells us, "I gave my attention to the Lord God to
seek Him by prayer and supplications, with fasting, sackcloth
and ashes" (Daniel 9:3). And notice how his prayer begins:
"Alas, O Lord, the great and awesome God, who keeps His
covenant and loving-kindness for those who love Him and keep
His commandments, we have sinned, committed iniquity, acted
wickedly and rebelled, even turning aside from Your commandments and ordinances" (vv. 4–5).

The starting point is praise. That gives way to penitence.
And as the prayer continues in Daniel 9, there are twelve more
verses of self-abasing confession as Daniel rehearses the sins of
Israel. It's filled with phrases like "Open shame belongs to us, O
Lord" (v. 8); "we have rebelled against Him; nor have we obeyed
the voice of the LORD our God" (vv. 9–10); and "we have
sinned, we have been wicked" (v. 15). Those expressions are
mingled with more praise: "Righteousness belongs to You, O
Lord, but to us open shame" (v. 7); "the LORD our God is

righteous with respect to all His deeds which He has done" (v. 14); and "[You] have brought Your people out of the land of Egypt with a mighty hand and have made a name for Yourself" (v. 15).

Finally, in the very last sentence of his prayer, Daniel makes *one request*, and it is a plea for mercy. All Daniel's praise (focusing on God's righteousness and His mercy) and all his penitence (outlining the history of Israel's disobedience) culminates in a prayer for forgiveness and restoration: "O Lord, hear! O Lord, forgive! O Lord, listen and take action! For Your own sake, O my God, do not delay, because Your city and Your people are called by Your name" (v. 19).

And that one request was preceded with this summary argument: Daniel gathered up all his praise and all his confession, condensed them all in one more affirmation of God's transcendent greatness and Israel's complete lack of merit, and then cited those very things as the grounds on which he was making his plea: "We are not presenting our supplications before You on account of any merits of our own, but on account of Your great compassion" (v. 18).

Again, notice that Daniel's prayer began with an affirmation of the nature and the glory and the greatness and the majesty of God. It is an expression of worship, and the request at the end thus flows from a worshipful, penitent heart. That is always the godly perspective.

Jonah prayed from the belly of a fish. If you can picture the wet, suffocating darkness and discomfort of such a place, you might begin to have an idea of how desperate Jonah's situation was at that moment. The whole second chapter of Jonah is devoted to the record of Jonah's prayer, and the entire prayer is a profound expression of worship. It reads like a psalm. In fact, it's full of references and allusions to the psalms—almost as if

Jonah were singing His worship in phrases borrowed from
Israel's psalter while he languished inside that living tomb.

The prayer is as passionate as you might expect from
someone trapped inside a fish under the surface of the
Mediterranean. Jonah begins: "I called out of my distress to the
LORD, and He answered me" (v. 2)—not a plea to God for help,
but an expression of praise and deliverance, mentioning God in
the third person and speaking of deliverance as if it were an
accomplished fact.

The remainder of the prayer is addressed directly to God in
the second person—and the whole thing is an extended
expression of more praise. Jonah rehearses what has happened
to him ("You had cast me into the deep," v. 3; "Weeds were
wrapped around my head," v. 5). Notice, Jonah is still inside the
fish while he is praying this prayer (cf. v. 10), yet he consistently
speaks of his deliverance in the past tense. And here's the
amazing thing about this prayer: Though Jonah must have been
as desperate as anyone who ever prayed for rescue from the
Lord, his prayer contains not one single *request*. It is a pure,
resounding expression of worship and faith in God, who alone
*could* deliver Jonah. The key sentence is verse 7: "While I was
fainting away, I remembered the LORD, and my prayer came to
You, into Your holy temple."

The focus of Jonah's prayer—like all great prayers—was the
glory of God. Although no one, perhaps, has ever been in a
situation where it would be more appropriate to plead and beg
God to answer, there was none of that in Jonah's prayer. And
the past-tense references to Jonah's deliverance were the furthest
thing you can imagine from the contemporary prosperity-
preachers' notion of "positive confession." Jonah wasn't under
any illusion that *his* words could alter the reality of his plight.
He was simply extolling the character of God. And that is

precisely what our Lord was teaching when He gave the disciples that model prayer in Luke 11.

So it ought to be clear that when Jesus taught His disciples to regard prayer as worship, that wasn't anything novel. The great prayers we read in the Old Testament were likewise expressions of worship—including those that were prayed in the most desperate situations.

With that in mind, look a little more closely now at Jesus' model prayer. The first verse of this prayer alone includes three truths that remind us our prayers are supposed to be expressions of worship.

### God's Paternity

The prayer starts with a reference to God's paternity. The first word—the address—is a reminder that God is our heavenly Father. We go to Him not only because He is a sovereign Monarch, a righteous Judge, and our Creator—but because He is a loving Father. That beautiful expression reminds us of the grace that gives us unlimited access to His throne (Hebrews 4:16)—and it encourages us to come boldly, just as a son or a daughter would come to a loving dad.

*That,* by the way, is the basis for our boldness in prayer. The point is not that our words have any kind of magical power, not that God is somehow obliged to give us whatever we ask for, and certainly not that our faith merits material rewards—but that God in His sovereignty invites us to come to Him as a gracious and loving Father. The intimacy of the Father-child relationship does not diminish the reverence we owe Him as our sovereign God. Far less does it give us any reason to exalt ourselves. Instead, it is a reminder that we should be childlike in our dependence on God's goodness and love. Ultimately, because He is our sovereign Lord, Creator, Judge, and Father, He is the only One on whom we can rely to supply all our needs and satisfy our deepest longings. If our prayers are truly worshipful, they will be permeated with recognition of that truth.

Take, for example, the prayer of Isaiah 64:8: "But now, O LORD, You are our Father, we are the clay, and You our potter; and all of us are the work of Your hand." That is the proper spirit of prayer: Lord, You made us. You gave us life. You alone can supply the resources we need. We are united with Your beloved Son by faith, and therefore we are Your children in every sense—totally dependent on Your will, Your power, and Your blessings.

That is very different from the prayer of a pagan who comes to a vengeful, violent, jealous, unjust, man-made deity, believing some merit or sacrifice must be brought to the altar to appease that hostile deity. The biblical perspective we bring to prayer is that God Himself offered the ultimate sacrifice and supplies all the merit we need in the Person of His Son. All who by faith lay hold of Christ as Lord and Savior are "sons of God" (Galatians 3:26; cf. John 1:12-13; 2 Corinthians 6:8). "See how great a love the Father has bestowed on us, that we would be called children of God; and such we are" (1 John 3:1).

In other words, the sacrifice of Christ was offered on our behalf, so we have already received the very best God has to give. And "He who did not spare His own Son, but delivered Him over for us all, how will He not also with Him freely give us all things?" (Romans 8:32).

As if that weren't enough, in Matthew 7:7-11, Jesus makes this promise: "Ask, and it will be given to you; seek, and you will find; knock, and it will be opened to you. For everyone who asks receives, and he who seeks finds, and to him who knocks it will be opened. Or what man is there among you who, when his son asks for a loaf, will give him a stone? Or if he asks for a fish, he will not give him a snake, will he? If you then, being evil, know how to give good gifts to your children, how much more will your Father who is in heaven give what is good to those who ask Him!"

So when we pray, we are going to a God who is our loving heavenly Father. We can go with a sense of intimacy. We can go with confidence, in the same tender, trusting way a little child would go to an earthly father. We can go boldly. We are approaching a loving deity who does not need to be appeased, but who embraces us as His own. In fact, because we are His true children, "God has sent forth the Spirit of His Son into our hearts, crying, 'Abba! Father!' " (Galatians 4:6). "Abba" is a term of deep affection, a common term for "father" derived from the Chaldean dialect. Because it is easy to pronounce, it was how little children in New Testament times commonly addressed their fathers, like "Daddy," or "Papa" in today's English.

But when we call God "Father," or "Abba," it is not a casual nod of crass, presumptuous, or easygoing familiarity. Used properly, "Abba"–"Father" is an expression of profound worship, filled with childlike trust: "God, I recognize that I'm Your child. I know You love me and have given me intimate access to You. I recognize that You have absolutely unlimited resources, and that You will do what is best for me. I recognize that I need to obey You. And I recognize that whatever You do, You know best." All of that is implied in the truth that God is our Father, and that's how Jesus taught us to begin our prayers.

Don't miss the point. When we pray to God as our heavenly Father, we are not only acknowledging our responsibility to obey Him, we are also confessing that He has a right to give us what He knows is best. Above all, we are offering Him praise and thanks for His loving grace, while confessing our own complete trust and dependence. In short, we are coming to Him as worshiping children—and *all* of that is implicit in the very first word of Jesus' model prayer.

## God's Priority

The entire opening sentence of the prayer is a straight-forward exclamation of worship: "Father, hallowed be Your name" (Luke 11:2). That is expressed as a petition, but it is by no means a personal request; it is an expression of praise, and it reflects God's own priority: "I am the LORD, that is My name; I will not give My glory to another" (Isaiah 42:8).

Jesus established the truth that prayer is worship by beginning His model prayer that way. To worship God is to "Sing the glory of His name" (Psalm 66:2). "Ascribe to the LORD the glory due His name" (1 Chronicles 16:29; Psalms 29:2; 96:8). "Not to us, O LORD, not to us, but to Your name give glory" (Psalm 115:1). Such expressions capture the true spirit of a worshiping heart.

Moreover, that first sentence qualifies every other petition in the prayer. It rules out asking for things "with wrong motives, so that you may spend it on your pleasures" (James 4:3). It eliminates every petition that is not in accord with the perfect will of God.

In the words of Arthur Pink:

> How clearly, then, is the fundamental duty in prayer here set forth: self and all its needs must be given a secondary place and the Lord freely accorded the preeminence in our thoughts, desires and supplications. This petition must take the precedence, for the glory of God's great name is the ultimate end of all things; every other request must not only be subordinated to this one, but be in harmony with and in pursuance of it. We cannot pray aright unless the honor of God be dominant in our hearts. If we cherish a desire for the honoring of God's name we must not ask for

anything which it would be against the Divine holiness to bestow.[3]

What does that expression mean: "Hallowed be Your name"? In biblical terms, God's "name" includes everything God is—His character, His attributes, His reputation, His honor—His very Person. God's name signifies everything that is true about God.

We still use the expression "my name" in that sense at times. If we say someone has ruined his good name, we mean he has disgraced himself and spoiled his reputation. He has diminished others' perception of who he is. And if I give you power of attorney, I have authorized you to act "in my name." You thereby become my legal proxy, and any legal covenants you enter into are as binding on me as if I signed them myself.

That is precisely what Jesus meant when He taught us to pray in His name: "Whatever you ask in My name, that will I do, so that the Father may be glorified in the Son. If you ask Me anything in My name, I will do it" (John 14:13-14). He was delegating His authority to us to be used in prayer—authorizing us to act as if we were His emissaries when we let our requests be made known to God.

But by teaching us to *begin* by asking that the name of God be hallowed, Christ put this built-in safeguard against the misuse of His name for our own self-aggrandizing purposes. If we truly want God's name to be hallowed, we would never sully the name of His Son or abuse the proxy He has given us by using His name to request that which He himself would never sanction. To do that would be to take His name in vain, and that is a violation of the third commandment. Furthermore,

---

[3] Arthur Pink, *The Sermon on the Mount* (Lafayette, IN: Sovereign Grace Publishers, 2001 reprint), 162.

immediately after Jesus delegated the authority of His name to His disciples, He said, "If you love Me, you will keep My commandments" (v. 15). He then restated the principle with all the necessary qualifications just one chapter later in John 16:7: *"If you abide in Me, and My words abide in you,* ask whatever you wish, and it will be done for you" (emphasis added).

It should be clear, then, that the expression "Your name" signifies far more than just a proper noun. God's name represents everything He is, everything He approves, and everything He is known for. So when we pray, "Father, hallowed be Your name," we are expressing a desire for God's character, His glory, His reputation in the world, and His very being to be set apart and lifted up.

The word *hallowed* (Greek *hagiazo*) means "consecrated," "sanctified," or "set apart as holy." It includes the idea of being separated from all that is profane. Putting it as simply as possible, this phrase is a prayer that God Himself would be blessed and glorified. Jesus Himself prayed for that very thing in John 12:28: "Father, glorify Your name." It is a petition God delights to answer.

By starting His model prayer that way, Jesus was reminding us of the ultimate purpose of every prayer we ever offer. The proper aim is for God to be glorified, exalted, honored, and known, in every conceivable way.

That, by the way, is a further reminder not to call God "Father" in a cheaply sentimental or overly familiar way. He is our loving Father, but we are not to forget that His name is Holy. The fatherhood of God in no way diminishes His glory, and if we find ourselves thinking that way here is the corrective: "Father, *hallowed be Your name.*"

The spirit of that plea is contrary to the main thrust of the so-called "prosperity gospel." I once heard a televangelist teaching the "positive confession" doctrine, and he told his audience that if they tacked the phrase "Not my will but thine" onto any of their prayers, they were not praying in faith. That is a lie from the pit of hell. Jesus Himself prayed, "not My will, but Yours be done" (Luke 22:42). By teaching us to begin all our prayers with a concern that the name of God to be hallowed, He was teaching us to pray for God's will over and above our own.

The kind of God who is at everyone's beck and call and who must knuckle under to someone else's desires is not the God of the Bible. Those who portray prayer in such a fashion are not hallowing God's name; they are dragging His name through the mud. Their false teaching is a denial of the very nature of God. It isn't just bad theology, it is gross irreverence. It is blasphemy. They are taking God's name in vain, and that is directly antithetical to the spirit of this plea.

Luther's catechism (section 39) asks and answers this question: "How is God's name hallowed among us? Answer, as plainly as it can be said: When both our doctrine and life are godly and Christian. For since in this prayer we call God our Father, it is our duty always to deport and demean ourselves as godly children, that He may not receive shame, but honor and praise from us."

So when we pray "Father, hallowed be Your name," we are asking God to glorify Himself—to put His power, His grace, and all His perfections on display. One way He does that is by answering our prayers—assuming our prayers are expressions of submission to His will rather than merely flippant requests that arise from our own selfish desires.

We were not created to enjoy prosperity in a fallen world. We were created to glorify God and enjoy *Him* forever. We ought to be more concerned for the glory of God than we are for our own prosperity, our own comfort, our own agenda, or any other self-centered desire. That's why Jesus taught us to think of prayer as an act of worship rather than merely a way to ask God for things we want.

### God's Program

The closing phrase of Luke 2 is "Your kingdom come." It is a prayer for the advancement of God's Kingdom. Like every phrase of the prayer we have looked at, this is antithetical to the prayers typically prayed by those who are concerned mainly about the advancement of their own program, the building of their own empire, or the padding of their own pockets. This is a prayer that *God's* program be advanced, and that *His* will be done. In fact, in some Greek manuscripts, the text includes the phrase, "Thy will be done, as in heaven, so in earth" (KJV). Jesus Himself included that phrase in the model prayer when he gave it in His Sermon on the Mount (Matthew 6:10).

Every request we make in our prayers should first be run through this filter: Is it in harmony with the goals and principles of God's kingdom? Is it consistent with the expansion of the Kingdom? Does it truly advance the Kingdom, or does it merely fulfill some selfish want?

"Name-it-and-claim-it" theology is myopic, self-indulgent, and small-minded. All it cares about is self-interest and selfish desires, with no thought for the greater cause of Christ's kingdom. The spirit of Christ says, "Lord, advance Your Kingdom if that means I lose everything." That's what the phrase "Your kingdom come" implies.

The kingdom, of course, is the sphere where Christ rules— the realm where He is Lord. To pray "Your kingdom come" with sincerity is to submit one's desires and to yield one's heart without reservation to the Lordship of Christ. To affirm the program of Christ's kingdom is to set aside one's own fleshly, materialistic, or selfish prayer requests because, after all, "the kingdom of God is not eating and drinking, but righteousness and peace and joy in the Holy Spirit" (Romans 14:17).

There is truly nothing wrong with praying to God for things we desire—as long as the desires of our heart are holy. Indeed, we are encouraged—repeatedly—to ask, and to trust, and to align our desires with the will of God. And we are promised answers to such prayers. "Delight yourself in the LORD; and He will give you the desires of your heart" (Psalm 37:4).

Remember, Jesus said, "If you abide in Me, and My words abide in you, ask whatever you wish, and it will be done for you" (John 15:7). "If you ask the Father for anything in My name, He will give it to you" (John 16:23). "This is the confidence which we have before Him, that, if we ask anything according to His will, He hears us" (1 John 5:14). Pay close attention to the qualifiers: "*If you abide in Me, and My words abide in you [then]* . . . whatever you wish." "Anything *in My name.*" "Anything *according to His will.*" Jesus' model prayer has those same qualifiers built into it because of the way He taught us to recognize God's paternity, yield to God's priority, and get on board with God's program *before we ever make one petition for ourselves.*

Any prayer that follows a different pattern is not an act of true worship, and therefore it is not a legitimate prayer.

Conversely, all true prayer *is* worship. We go to a loving Father, accepting that He knows best. Our prayers, then, reflect an obedient heart, a passion for His glory, and a desire to see the extension of His Kingdom—that God might be honored.

# God-Centered Prayer
## John Piper
### Matthew 6:5-15

[5] And when you pray, you must not be like the hypocrites. For they love to stand and pray in the synagogues and at the street corners, that they may be seen by others. Truly, I say to you, they have received their reward. [6] But when you pray, go into your room and shut the door and pray to your Father who is in secret. And your Father who sees in secret will reward you. [7] And when you pray, do not heap up empty phrases as the Gentiles do, for they think that they will be heard for their many words. [8] Do not be like them, for your Father knows what you need before you ask Him. [9] Pray then like this:

> Our Father in heaven, hallowed be Thy name.
> [10] Thy kingdom come, Thy will be done, on earth
>   as it is in heaven.
> [11] Give us this day our daily bread,
> [12] and forgive us our debts, as we also have forgiven
>   our debtors.
> [13] And lead us not into temptation, but deliver us from
>   evil.
> [14] For if you forgive others their trespasses, your heavenly
>   Father will also forgive you,
> [15] but if you do not forgive others their trespasses, neither
>   will your Father forgive your trespasses.

I love the prayers of the Bible. They shape my own prayers more than anything else. I love the prayers of Paul in Philippians 1:9-11, in Ephesians 1:16-21 and 3:14-19, and Colossians

1:9-12. I love the prayer of Jesus in John 17. And I love the whole book of Psalms, which is the inspired prayer book of the church, filled with such a range of emotions that the cry of our heart in almost any experience can find words in the Psalms.

But the prayer in the Bible that gripped me most during a leave of absence I once took is the Lord's Prayer in Matthew 6:9-13. This is probably because, in God's providence, I was memorizing the Sermon on the Mount with many of my congregation. So week after week I was reviewing Matthew 6 in my mind, and so saying the Lord's Prayer over and over.

As I thought about it and prayed it, it had an effect on the big picture of my life, and it had an effect on the nitty-gritty, daily wrestlings in my life. I hope it will have a similar effect on you as you pray it.

The Lord's Prayer is very true to life in this sense. Life is a combination of spectacular things and simple things. In almost everyone's life there are breath-taking things and boring things, fantastic things and familiar things, extraordinary things and ordinary things, awesome things and average things, exotic things and everyday things. That's the way life is.

And, looked at it in one way, that's the way the Lord's Prayer is. Almost everyone notices that it has two parts. The first part (verses 9-10) has three petitions; and the second part (verses 11-13) has three petitions. The first three petitions are:

    * Hallowed be Thy name
    * Thy kingdom come
    * Thy will be done on earth as it is in heaven.

We are asking God to bring about these three things: Cause your name to be hallowed, cause your kingdom to come, and cause your will to be done as it's done by the angels in heaven.

The second three petitions are:

    * Give us this day our daily bread

\* Forgive us our debts, as we also have forgiven our debtors

\* Lead us not into temptation, but deliver us from evil.

You can see the difference—and feel the difference—between these two halves. The first three petitions are about God's name, God's kingdom, and God's will. The last three are about our food, our forgiveness, and our holiness. The first three call our attention to God's greatness. And the last three call attention to our needs. The two halves have a very different feel. The first half feels majestic and lofty. The last half feels mundane and lowly.

In other words, there is a correspondence between the content of this prayer and the content of our lives—the big and the little, the glorious and the common, the majestic and the mundane, the lofty and the lowly.

Ecclesiastes 3:11 says, "God has put eternity into man's heart, yet so that he cannot find out what God has done from the beginning to the end." I take that to mean that the world and the human soul are iridescent with wonders linked to eternity. And yet our humdrum, ordinary, mundane experiences in this world keep us from seeing the wonders and from soaring the way we dream from time to time. Even we believers who are indwelt by the Holy Spirit of God, even we say, "We have this treasure in jars of clay" (2 Corinthians 4:7). Our spirit is alive with God's Spirit, but our bodies are dead because of sin (Romans 8:10).

That's the way life is. And that's the way this prayer is—iridescent with eternity and woven into ordinary life.

I see a great deal in these verses. Let me paraphrase:

\* Verse 9: Father, cause your great and holy name to be honored and reverenced and esteemed and treasured above all things everywhere in the world (including my heart).

\* Verse 10: And cause your glorious, sovereign, kingly rule to hold sway without obstruction everywhere in the world (including my heart).

\* Verse 10: And cause your all-wise, all-good, all-just, all-holy will to be done all over this world the way the angels do it perfectly and joyfully in heaven—and make it happen in me.

That's the breathtaking part of the prayer. And when we pray it we are caught up into great things, glorious things, global things, and eternal things. God wants this to happen. He wants your life to be enlarged like that, enriched like that, expanded and ennobled and soaring like that.

But then we pray,

\* Verse 11: Father, I am not asking for the bounty of riches. I am asking for bread, just enough to give me life. I want to live. I want to be healthy, and to have a body and a mind that work. Would you give me what I need for my body and mind?

\* Verse 12: And, Father, I am a sinner and need to be forgiven every day. I can't live and flourish with guilt. I will die if I have to bear my guilt every day. I have no desire to hold any grudge. I know I don't deserve forgiveness, and so I have no right to withhold it from anyone. I let go of all the offenses against me. Please, have mercy upon me and forgive me and let me live in the freedom of your love. And, of course, we know now what Jesus knew when He said this. He knew he would also say of His death: "This is My blood of the covenant, which is poured out for many for the forgiveness of sins" (Matthew 26:28). When we pray for forgiveness, we expect it not merely because God is our Father, but because our Father gave His Son to die in our place.

\* Verse 13: And Father, I don't want to go on sinning. I'm thankful for forgiveness, but, Father, I don't want to sin. Please, don't lead me into the entanglements of overpowering temptation. Deliver me from evil. Guard me from Satan and from all his works and all his ways. Grant me to walk in holiness.

That's the earthy part of the prayer. The mundane, daily, nitty-gritty struggle of the Christian life. We need food and forgiveness and protection from evil.

I think the two halves of this great prayer correspond to the two things said about God in the way Jesus tells us to address Him at the beginning in verse 9: "Our Father—in heaven." First, God is a Father to us. And, second, He is infinitely above us and over all—in heaven. His fatherhood corresponds to His readiness to meet our earthly needs. His heavenliness corresponds to His supreme right to be given worship and allegiance and obedience.

For example, in Matthew 6:32 Jesus tells us not to be anxious about food and drink and clothing because "your heavenly Father knows that you need them all." In other words, Jesus wants us to feel the fatherhood of God as an expression of His readiness to meet our most basic needs.

And then consider Matthew 5:34, where Jesus says, "Do not take an oath. . .by heaven, for it is the throne of God." In other words, when you think of heaven, think of God's throne, His kingly majesty and power and authority.

So when Jesus tells us in Matthew 6:9 to pray, "Our Father in heaven," He is telling us that the prayer-hearing God is majestic and merciful. He is high, and also dwells with the contrite (Isaiah 57:15). He is a King and He is a Father. He is holy and He humbles Himself. He is far above us, and ready to come to us. He has plans for the whole earth and for the universe, and wants us to care about these great plans and pray about them; and He has plans for your personal life at the most practical level and wants you to pray about that.

So on October 5th last year, I wrote in my journal:

"My heart's desire is to be used by God for the hallowing of His name and the coming of His kingdom and the doing of His will.

To that end I pray for:
>     Health—give me daily bread;
>     Hope—forgive my debts; and
>     Holiness—deliver me from evil."

In other words, it seems to me that the great designs of God are first and mainly about God—His name being hallowed, His will being done, His kingdom coming. And the rest of the prayer is how I can be fitted to serve those great designs. My bread, my forgiveness, my deliverance—my health, my hope, my holiness—are for the purpose of being part of God's great purposes to glorify His name and exalt His rule and complete His will.

But there was one more exegetical insight that came as I pondered and prayed this prayer again and again during my leave of absence. There is something unique about the first petition, "Hallowed be Thy name." It's not just one of three. In this petition we hear the one specific, subjective response of the human heart that God expects us to give—the hallowing, reverencing, honoring, esteeming, admiring, valuing, and treasuring of God's name above all things. None of the other five requests tells us to pray for a specific human response of the heart.

If you combine this fact with the fact that this petition comes first, and that the "name" of God ("hallowed be Thy name") is more equivalent to the being of God than is His kingdom or His will, my conclusion is that this petition is the main point of the prayer and all the others are meant to serve this one.

In other words, the structure of the prayer is not merely that the last three petitions serve the first three, but that the last five serve the first.

So on October 9th last year, I wrote in my journal:

"My ONE Great Passion!

Nothing is more clear and unshakeable to me than that the purpose of the universe is for the hallowing of God's name.

His kingdom comes for THAT.

His will is done for THAT.

Humans have bread-sustained life for THAT.

Sins are forgiven for THAT.

Temptation is escaped for THAT."

And then on the next day, October 10th, I wrote:

"Lord, grant that I would, in all my weaknesses and limitations, remain close to the one clear, grand theme of my life: Your magnificence."

Here is the sum of the matter. Sooner or later life almost overwhelms you with pressures and problems—physical problems (give us daily bread), relational and mental problems (forgive us our debts), moral problems (lead us not into temptation). And what I want you to see is this: You have a Father. He is a thousand times better as a Father than the best human father. His fatherhood means that He cares about every one of those problems, and He beckons you to talk to Him about them in prayer and to come to Him for help. He knows what you need (Matthew 6:32).

That's the way we usually attack our problems. And so we should. We attack them directly. "I have this financial problem, or this relational problem, or this bad habit problem. Father, help me." That is right and good.

But Jesus offers us more in this prayer. There is more—not less than that, but more. There is an indirect attack on our problems. There is a remedy—not a complete deliverance from all problems in this life, but a powerful remedy—in the first three petitions of the Lord's Prayer, especially the first one.

God made you to be a part of hallowing His name, extending His kingdom, and seeing His will done on the earth the way the angels do it in heaven. In other words, He made you for something magnificent and for something mundane. He made you for something spectacular and for something simple. He loves both. He honors both. But what we often fail to see is that when we lose our grip on the greatness of God, and His name and His kingdom and His global will, we lose our divine equilibrium in life, and we are far more easily overwhelmed by the problems of the mundane.

In other words, I am pleading with you not to lose your grip on the supremacy and centrality of hallowing the name of God in your life. I am urging you from the Lord's prayer that you go to God for bread, and for healing of relationships, and for the overcoming of besetting sins, and for the doing of God's will, and for the seeking of God's kingdom—all of it, all the time, for the sake of knowing and hallowing, reverencing, honoring, valuing, and treasuring God's name (God's being, God Himself) above all things.

Keep your feet on the ground. That's why the second three petitions are there. But let your heart rise into the magnificence of God's global will, God's kingdom, and, most of all, God's holy name—His being, His perfections.

You may not see it clearly now, but I testify from the Scriptures and from experience, there is more deliverance, more healing, more joy in the hallowing of His name than perhaps you ever dreamed. Let's pray always in the fullness of this prayer.

# Hallowing God's Name
## Joel Beeke

"Hallowed be Thy name." Matthew 6:9b

"Father, glorify Thy name." John 12:28

"Grant us, first, rightly to know Thee, and to sanctify, glorify, and praise Thee in all Thy works, in which Thy power, wisdom, goodness, justice, mercy and truth, are clearly displayed; and further also, that we may so order and direct our whole lives, our thoughts, words and actions, that Thy name may never be blasphemed, but rather honored and praised on our account."
Heidelberg Catechism, Q. 122

What's in a name? Much indeed! Shakespeare's Juliet argues that "a rose by any other name would smell as sweet," but names cannot change reality. A rose is still a rose even if you call it a dandelion. And if you go into a flower shop and order a dozen dandelions, don't expect to impress your wife. Names are important. Calling something by the wrong name can lead others astray, especially if it's the name of a road and you are the one giving directions.

We live in a time when names often have little significance. This is evident in the names that some people give their children. They tend to give children names that sound nice and are popular. In England, lists of the ten most popular names for daughters include Sarah, not because it was the name God gave to Abraham's wife, hailed in Scripture as a holy woman who trusted in God (1 Peter 3:5-6), but because of Sarah Ferguson,

Duchess of York and former wife of Prince Andrew. It appears that many people no longer give due consideration to the meaning or historical importance of a name.

It was not so in Bible times. Parents often named their children according to what they hoped or even feared those children would one day become. Sometimes parents named a child after a particular attribute of God, hoping that God would reveal Himself that way in the child's life. So, in the case of the four "children of Judah" of Daniel 1:6, Daniel means "God is my Judge"; Hananiah, "the LORD shows grace"; Mishael, "Who is what God is?"; and Azariah, "the LORD helps." On the other hand, the name Nabal–the husband of Abigail as recorded in 1 Samuel 25– means "fool" (v. 25; cf. v. 3d). Judging by the man's words and actions, he was indeed a very foolish man, one whose folly put all his household and possessions at risk.

If I ask you to think of your best friend, you most likely will think first of that person's name, then of certain physical characteristics or personality traits. He or she may be tall or short, blonde or brunette, stocky or lean, grumpy or happy, talkative or shy, a good sport or a sore loser, dour or funny, but the name remains the same.

The name of the person and his character or behavior, then, can be linked. Some of us name our sons after men of renown because we would like to see them live up to that name and what it represents. Think of David, the man after God's own heart (1 Samuel 13:14; Acts 13:22); Peter, the rock (Matthew 16:18); or John, meaning "the Lord is gracious" (Luke 1:13). Today parents still name their sons Paul, after the great apostle. On the other hand, the name of Nero, the emperor whom had Paul put to death, is given to a dog.

What is true of human names is infinitely truer of God's name. God's name refers to His being or essence, His perfec-

tions, and His works. James Fisher says that God's name includes "every thing by which He is pleased to make himself
known," including His names, titles, attributes, ordinances,
Word, and works.[1] When God revealed Himself to Moses as "I
AM THAT I AM" (Exodus 3:14), He was revealing His covenant
name (Jehovah) by which He wished to be known and worshipped in Israel. This name expresses the nature and character
of God as eternal, unchanging and unchangeable, ever faithful,
covenant-keeping, and altogether worthy of the full trust of His
people. This "immortal, invisible, only-wise God" (1 Timothy
1:17) has revealed Himself most fully in His Son, Jesus Christ,
"the same yesterday, and today, and forever" (Hebrews 13:8; cf.
Psalm 72:17).

The name of God also reveals Him as defender of His people—"The LORD hear thee in the day of trouble; the name of the
God of Jacob defend thee" (Psalm 20:1)—and as a place of ref-
uge. "The name of the LORD is a strong tower; the righteous
runneth into it, and is safe," says Proverbs 18:10. His people
trust in that name. Isaiah 50:10 says: "Let him trust in the name
of the LORD, and stay upon his God." His people love God's
name (Psalm 69:36), fear God's name (Malachi 4:2), call upon
God's name (Zephaniah 3:9), and bless God's name (Psalm
100:4).

The name of God also refers to His reputation. Proverbs
22:1 states: "A good name is rather to be chosen than great
riches." James Fisher wrote that a good name is "the having of
reputation and esteem, especially among the sober and religious
(Psalm 16:3 and 101:6)."[2] Just as a man should be zealous to
maintain a good name in the community, God acts to protect

---

[1] James Fisher, *The Assembly's Shorter Catechism Explained* (Stoke-on-Trent,
U.K.: Berith Publications, 1998), 272; cf., Shorter Catechism, Q. 54.
[2] Fisher, *Shorter Catechism Explained*, 336; cf. Shorter Catechism, Q. 77.

His own reputation in the eyes of the world. So after the terrible defeat suffered at the hands of the men of Ai, Joshua appeals to God, saying, "O Lord, what shall I say, when Israel turneth their backs before their enemies. . .and what wilt Thou do unto Thy great name?" (Joshua 7:8-9).

The most fundamental act of faith and worship is described in Scripture as "calling upon the name of the LORD" (Genesis 4:26; Romans 10:11-13). When we call upon the name of the LORD, we call upon everything that God is—all that He has revealed Himself to be, all that He has done for the salvation of His people, and all that He has promised to do for us in Christ. This is why we dare not take the name of God upon our lips except with the deepest reverence.

When our Lord Jesus Christ taught us to pray, He began on a glorious note: "Our Father which art in heaven, hallowed be Thy name" (Matthew 6:9b). These words, known as the preface or address of the Lord's Prayer, establish a priority for all true prayer in terms of the proper starting point. Christ teaches us to begin with God, with who He is, and the things that matter most to Him.

### The Priority in Prayer

If I asked you to write down what is most important to God, what would you write? According to Jesus, the list should include God's fatherly love, His heavenly glory, His holy name, His eternal kingdom, and His righteous will. Those concerns ought to be our starting point in prayer, Jesus says. Instead of beginning prayer with a reference to what is important to us at the moment—a sickness to be healed, a financial need to be met, or some other problem in life to be solved—we should start with what is most important to God. This does not mean that our needs are unimportant. God is ever mindful of us (Psalm 8:4), shares in all our afflictions (Isaiah 63:9), and cares for us (1 Peter 5:7) with a father's tender love (Psalm 103:13). Nevertheless, the name and honor of God is so overriding that this must be our primary focus, especially in prayer.

A great danger is to ignore God's primacy, even while talking to Him. The first petition of the Lord's Prayer, "Hallowed be Thy name," reminds us how often our prayers are man-centered. Though self-centered prayers seem to address our needs, in reality they do not satisfy, for our greatest need is to know God and to show His glory to the world. To aim our prayers at anything less is to exchange our high calling as God's image-bearers and children for the role of mere clients in search of a service provider. It asks for mud instead of gold.

In this first petition, Jesus Christ teaches us that a profound sense of God's glorious holiness and perfection must fill us at the very beginning of prayer. It is vital to extol God's glory in all our prayers. I was deeply impressed on a trip to Northern Ireland with the prayers of several Christians I met there. The first half of their prayers was often devoted to recounting the attributes of God and praising Him as Creator, Provider, and Redeemer. They were God-centered prayers, praising Him and worshipping Him, just as David does in Psalm 145. Joseph A. Alexander comments on this psalm: "In form it is an alphabetical [acrostic] psalm. . .being made up of variations on a single theme, the righteousness and goodness of the Lord to men in general, to His own people in particular, and more especially to those who suffer."[3] The entire psalm is one of praise, extolling God and hallowing His Name. We must do likewise when we approach God in prayer. We must pray that His reputation and

---

[3] Joseph A. Alexander, *The Psalms Translated and Explained* (repr., Grand Rapids: Baker Book House, 1975), 553.

honor will be promoted in our lives, in the church, and in the world, where it is so often trampled underfoot.

**Petition, Not Mere Description or Praise**

When we say, "Hallowed be Thy name," this is not to be understood as a sentence in the indicative. We are not merely saying, "God, Thy name is holy." Rather, we are using the imperative, calling upon God to act. In the Greek form of this and other petitions, the verb comes first. These petitions literally say, "Cause Thy name to be hallowed. Cause Thy kingdom to come. Cause Thy will to be done." In each case, we may add, "in earth, as it is in heaven."

The verbs are reverent imperatives, earnest entreaties, serious requests made of the Lord by His servants. The verbs are passive in voice, indicating not an intention on our part to do something, but rather imploring God to act, acknowledging that without Him we can do nothing (John 15:5). We are asking God to do these things; we are not volunteering to do them for Him. Of course, we cannot sincerely offer such prayers and not do all we can to hallow His name, promote the coming of His kingdom, and do His will. But the point of the prayer is not to declare what we think or promise to do; we are pressing God to arise and "cause Thyself to be known here on earth as Thou art known in heaven."

What, specifically, are we asking God to do when we pray, "Hallowed be Thy name?" The Heidelberg Catechism (Q. 122) expounds the first petition of the Lord's Prayer, "Hallowed be Thy name," in these terms: "Grant us, first, rightly to know Thee, and to sanctify, glorify, and praise Thee in all Thy works, in which Thy power, wisdom, goodness, justice, mercy and truth, are clearly displayed; and further also, that we may so order and direct our whole lives, our thoughts, words and actions, that Thy Name may never be blasphemed, but honored and praised on our account."

In this petition we are asking God to grant us three things: "first, rightly to know Thee"; second, for the will and ability "to sanctify, magnify and praise Thee"; and third, for the direction and help that we need "that we may so order and direct our whole lives, our thoughts, words and actions" for His glory. In other words, we are praying to our Father that He would make His name known to mankind, move men to reverence His name, and teach men to order the whole of their lives for the honor and praise of His name.

### Our Father, Grant Us to Know Thee Rightly

To hallow God's name, we must know who He is. In this context, "to hallow" means "to honor as holy."[4] We must be able to recognize God's holiness before we can see it in His name; and only God can make Himself known to us. So the Catechism interprets the petition as first of all the expression of a hunger to know God as He truly is: "Grant us, first, rightly to know Thee."

How can we rightly know God? The Catechism speaks of knowing God in "all Thy works, in which Thy power, wisdom, goodness, justice, mercy and truth, are clearly displayed." God's works reveal both His power and His goodness. The Psalms abound with this truth. "The heavens declare the glory of God; and the firmament showeth His handiwork" (Psalm 19:1). As we gaze upon the majesty of God's creation, how can we not be overcome with praise?

All people are aware of God's creation, says the Apostle Paul. "For the invisible things of Him from the creation of the

---

[4] *Concise Oxford Dictionary*, 4th ed. (Oxford: University Press, 1952), 545.

world are clearly seen, being understood by the things that are made, even His eternal power and Godhead" (Romans 1:20). But do people praise God for His eternal power and Godhead? No, they hold or suppress the truth in unrighteousness. They neither glorify God nor give Him thanks. They worship the creature rather than the Creator (Romans 1:21-25).

By the grace of God, the Christian's tongue has been loosed to sing the praises of his Maker. When the Holy Spirit renews the hearts and minds of God's people, their eyes are opened to see the beauty and power of God's handiwork in the splendor of a sunrise, the majesty of a mountain, the swift flight of an eagle swooping down in search of prey, or the undulations of vast prairies as the wind stirs the grass. The child of God looks upon all of this and exclaims, "This is the handiwork of my Father in heaven—hallowed be Thy name!"

But God's greatest work is not creation; rather, it is the redemption of the world through Jesus Christ. When we pray, "Our Father which art in heaven, hallowed be Thy name," we are echoing the prayer of God's own Son. As the hour of His death approached, with a troubled soul Christ prayed, "Father, glorify Thy name" (John 12:28). Later, in the upper room, He prayed again, "Father, the hour is come; glorify Thy Son, that Thy Son also may glorify Thee, as Thou hast given Him power over all flesh, that He should give eternal life to as many as Thou hast given Him. And this is life eternal, that they might know Thee, the only true God, and Jesus Christ, whom Thou hast sent" (John 17:1-3). In the body of His "high priestly prayer," Christ invokes His Father's name four times: As the sum of all the truth Christ manifested and declared to the disciples until that hour and afterwards by His death and resurrection, and as the power in which Christ had kept the disciples while He was with them and by which they and those who should believe on Christ through their word would be kept in the world (John 17:6, 11, 12, 26). Christ calls on God as "Holy Father" and "Righteous Father" (John 17:11, 25). Finally, Christ asks the Father to sanctify or hallow the disciples through the truth of His Word, even as Christ has sanctified Himself (John 17:17, 19). In all these ways this prayer of Jesus is linked to our petition, "Our Father which art in heaven, Hallowed be Thy name."

At the same time, Christ prayed, "Glorify Thy Son, that Thy Son also may glorify Thee" (John 17:1). The Father honors His name by honoring His Son. We should think here of Christ's exaltation to the right hand of God, of His certain mediatorial glory promised to Him in the counsel of the Trinity before time began (John 17:5, 24). "Wherefore God also hath highly exalted Him, and given Him a name which is above every name, that at the name of Jesus every knee should bow, of things in heaven, and things in earth, and things under the earth; and that every tongue should confess that Jesus Christ is Lord, to the glory of God the Father" (Philippians 2:5-11). Christ's exaltation as Lord glorifies the Father. When we pray to the Father, "Hallowed be Thy name," we also pray for God to make known to us and to people everywhere the glory of the Lord Jesus, our heavenly Prophet, Priest, and King, the "one mediator between God and men" (1 Timothy 2:5).

But Christ's prayer for the Father to glorify Him also encompasses His sufferings and death. John 13:31 tells us that when Judas left the upper room to betray Him, Jesus said, "Now is the Son of man glorified, and God is glorified in Him." In the darkest hours of our Lord's life, when He was betrayed and forsaken, tried and condemned, spitefully used and rejected of men, led away to be crucified and put to death, His glory blazed brightly. Ultimately God revealed His name in a perfect way on

Calvary's cross. On the one hand, He revealed His justice in the punishment of sin; on the other, He commended His love in delivering up His Son to death for the salvation of sinners.

How beautifully and judiciously God harmonized all His attributes through His Son's sacrifice on Calvary! His death on the cross displays the paradoxical grandeur of suffering and shame, greatness and glory. At Calvary infinite goodness and infinite justice met together and were satisfied in the person and work of the Lord Jesus Christ. "Mercy and truth are met together; righteousness and peace have kissed each other" (Psalm 85:10). Alexander writes: "God's mercy or free favor to the undeserving is now seen to be consistent with His truth, which was pledged for their destruction, and their peace or safety, with His righteousness or justice, which might otherwise have seemed to be wholly incompatible."[5]

The worshipper at the foot of the cross is humbled and filled with wonder as he gazes upon Emmanuel, the "express image" of God (Hebrews 1:3) now "come in the flesh" (1 John 4:2). At the cross we may say, as nowhere else in the world, "Hallowed be Thy name." We long for the entire world to see God's glory in Christ. Indeed, we pray for the entire world to see the glory of the cross. In so doing, we must pray that the gospel may be preached to all people, in the illuminating and convicting power of the Spirit, so that "all the ends of the world shall remember and turn unto the LORD: and all kindreds of the nations shall worship before Thee" (Psalm 22:27).

Christ prayed, "Glorify Thy Son, that Thy Son also may glorify Thee." How was the Father glorified when Christ was glorified? Christ answers this question: "As Thou hast given Him power over all flesh, that He should give eternal life to as many

---

[5] Alexander, *The Psalms Translated*, 360; cf. Romans 3:23–26.

as Thou hast given Him." Christ's exaltation as Lord "over all flesh" enables Him to give eternal life to all the elect of God. In giving eternal life to these favored sinners, Christ shows them the glory of His Father. He taught us this in John 17:3: "And this is life eternal, that they might know Thee the only true God, and Jesus Christ, whom Thou hast sent."

Do you see the logic? When the Father glorified His Son through His death and resurrection, His Son was then positioned to give eternal life to the elect, and eternal life consists of knowing God. Through Jesus Christ the elect see the Father's love and righteousness; they know the Father's majesty and mercy. Therefore "Hallowed be Thy name" is an evangelistic and missionary prayer, for God has forever bound the glory of His name to the work of His Son in redeeming sinners. When we pray this petition, our hearts should thrill with the knowledge that the gospel will go forth into the entire world, to all people, and to all the elect of God.

"Hallowed be Thy name" is not a vague prayer to a generic deity. It can only be prayed rightly by faith in Christ. This first petition says, "Cause Thy name to be central by having people acknowledge Thee as Christ has revealed Thee." Jesus says that no man knows the Father except the Son, and he to whom the Son chooses to reveal Him (Matthew 11:27). Faithfulness to the gospel as proclaimed by Christ requires us to say in direct and simple terms that there is only one way to know God rightly—through the person and work of His Son, Jesus Christ. Anyone who claims to know God another way is worshipping an idol, not the true and living God.

The exclusiveness of Christianity is offensive to many who espouse the values of multiculturalism in a pluralistic society. Religious liberty is a great blessing, but pluralism is more than religious liberty. Philosophical pluralism demands that we tolerate as equally valid multiple and even contradictory theological understandings and religious practices. Have Christians today capitulated so much to this kind of pluralism that we are unwilling to assert the exclusiveness of the names and claims of God as revealed in Jesus Christ? Most of us even have difficulty getting to the point of the gospel and telling people, lovingly and firmly, that unless they repent and believe in Jesus, they are heading for eternal damnation. When we pray, "Hallowed be Thy name," we must understand that the name of God represents God as He truly is, not as people imagine Him to be. In a world where the truth of God has been changed into a lie (Romans 1:25), we cry out, "Hallowed be Thy name! Make Thy glory known through Thy Son!" That is the first implication of this petition.

### Our Father, Move Us to Magnify Thee

Bare knowledge that does not move the heart does not hallow God's name. God seeks worshippers who worship Him not just in truth, but also in spirit (John 4:24), that is, with their spirits animated and moved by truth that is inspired and illuminated by His Spirit. So the Catechism says that in this first petition we pray that God would also move us "to hallow, magnify, and praise" Him as He works in us "both to will and to do of His good pleasure" (Philippians 2:13).

To magnify in this context means to "extol,"[6] that is, to praise God by proclaiming the greatness of His power, the glory of His kingdom, the steadfastness of His love, the depth of His mercy, and the riches of His grace; in a word, to declare the *magnificence* of God. David does this in Psalm 34:1–3, saying, "I will bless the LORD at all times. His praise shall continually be in

---

[6] *Concise Oxford Dictionary*, 720.

my mouth. My soul shall make her boast in the LORD; the humble shall hear thereof, and be glad. O magnify the LORD with me, and let us exalt His name together." Rightly knowing the Lord moves the believer to honor God as God and lift up His holy name in thankful praise. Hallowing God's name involves trusting in Him, loving Him, doing His will, and confessing His name as "the LORD who made heaven and earth" (Psalm 124:8).

Scriptural terms such as "magnify" or "glorify" may suggest an attempt to add significance to God's name. But God doesn't need us to pray for Him or to add to His glory. He is supremely glorious in Himself. We cannot add to His intrinsic glory, but we are called to live out our faith in a visible way, "before men, that they may see your good works, and glorify your Father which is in heaven" (Matthew 5:15). So when we pray "Hallowed be Thy name," we are asking for grace to honor His holiness in our families, our churches, our nation, and our world.

With this first petition of the Lord's Prayer we are also asking the Father to enable us to worship Him in spirit and in truth, both in public and private worship. Too much of what passes for worship today hardly mentions God, His attributes, His mighty works, or His holy wrath against sin. Contemporary worship focuses on us and our feelings. Scripture teaches us a very different way to worship God. We are commanded to sing the Psalms (Psalm 47:6, 7; 95:2; 105:2), which are full of God-centered worship:

> His holy Name remember, ye saints, Jehovah praise;
> His anger lasts a moment, His favor all our days.
>
> All glory, might, and honor ascribe to God on high;
> His arm protects His people who on His pow'r rely.
> Forth from Thy holy dwelling Thy awful glories shine;

Thou strengthenest Thy people; unending praise be Thine.

Not unto us, O Lord of heav'n, but unto Thee be glory giv'n;
In love and truth Thou dost fulfill the counsels of Thy sov'reign
    will;
Though nations fail Thy pow'r to own, yet Thou dost reign, and
    Thou alone.[7]

Private and family worship can also benefit from singing
God-centered hymns such as this one, written by Isaac Watts:

Eternal Power, whose high abode
Becomes the grandeur of a God,
Infinite length beyond the bounds
Where stars revolve their little rounds....

Lord, what shall earth and ashes do?
We would adore our Maker, too;
From sin and dust to Thee we cry,
The Great, the Holy, and the High![8]

Are you troubled by the fact that the name of God is not
central in much public worship today? The name of our God
isn't even known in many parts of our world. Instead, other
gods are implored of, worshipped, and praised. Are you zealous
of the name of God? A day is coming when Jesus will bring His
redemptive work to its culmination, and the name of God will
finally be honored as it ought. That will truly be a great day.
One of the deepest yearnings of the people of God is that the
name of God is honored, and that God, as He truly is, and all

---

[7] Selections from *The Psalter* (Grand Rapids: Reformation Heritage Books,
1999), Nos. 77:2; 183:4; 308:1.
[8] *An Arrangement of the Psalms, Hymns, and Spiritual Songs of the Rev. Isaac
Watts*, ed. James M. Winchell (Boston: James Loring, 1832), Hymn #38.

that His name represents, be known, believed, and honored throughout the earth.

You may sometimes pray, "Lord, my grandma is unsaved. Remove the darkness from her eyes and let the glory of the gospel in the face of Jesus Christ shine into her mind and enable her to repent and believe. Open her heart so that she worships Thee with the love Thou dost so richly deserve." What is really most important is that when you pray that prayer, you are praying that the name of God will be made central in the world. If Grandma believes, the fame and reputation of our God will be extended and His name will be made central because God will have moved her from the kingdom of darkness to Jesus Christ, the only true revelation of God. If Grandma believes, God's name, fame, and reputation will be extended in the world. Is that the supreme reason why you desire the salvation of those whom you love?

When you read the Lord's Prayer, you might wonder why we do not petition God to save sinners and bless the missionaries. Yet we do. When we pray that God's name be hallowed, we are asking that His name, fame, and reputation will be honored in the world. The goal of evangelism and missions is to produce spiritually-quickened, well-instructed, heartfelt worshippers of the true God. Is God the center of your life? This petition says, "Cause Thy name, cause Thyself to be adored as God under all the skies of the earth. Cause Thy name, Thy fame, Thy reputation to shine forth," not just here in our home, our church, and our country, but over the *whole earth*. When the earth is full of the knowledge of the LORD (Isaiah 11:9), the glory of the LORD will be revealed (Isaiah 40:5), and mankind will cry aloud with the seraphim, "Holy, holy, holy, is the LORD of hosts: the whole earth is full of his glory" (Isaiah 6:4).

So the second implication of this petition is that we pray for God to gather worshippers to Himself and that He would be known and acknowledged as God in all His power, wisdom, goodness, justice, mercy, and truth. We are asking God to move people to praise Him as God.

**Our Father, Order Our Lives for Thy Honor**
The Catechism goes on to say, ". . .and further also, [grant] that we may so order and direct our whole lives, our thoughts, words and actions, that Thy Name may never be blasphemed, but rather honored and praised on our account." This petition embraces all that God is and all that He does, as well as the totality of who we are and all that we do. In our works, thoughts, words, and actions we are called to hallow God as Creator, Redeemer, and Sanctifier.

Do you hallow God in your thoughts? Can you say with the psalmist, "My meditation of Him shall be sweet" (Psalm 104:34)? You can't possibly hallow God's name in your thoughts if you don't ever think of God. Do you hallow God with your words? You can't possibly hallow God's name if you don't speak of Him wherever you go, using "the holy name of God no otherwise than with fear and reverence."[9] Do you hallow God in your actions, resolving "to live, not only according to some, but all the commandments of God?"[10] Do you sanctify the Lord God of hosts by letting Him be your fear (Isaiah 8:13)? Do you serve Him with childlike fear (Hebrews 12:9)? You can't possibly honor God with your actions without childlike faith and submission, godly fear, and joyous thankfulness. To so order and direct our whole lives that God's name may be honored and

---

[9] Heidelberg Catechism, Q. 99.
[10] Heidelberg Catechism, Q. 114.

praised on our account, we also need guidance and assistance, the guidance of the Word and Spirit of God, and the assistance of His grace.

Does your life validate your prayers? Or do you pray for God's name to be hallowed while living an unhallowed life? Is your life marked by actions that hallow God's name, such as repentance from sin, heartfelt trust, conscientious obedience to His Word, and unstinting thankfulness? Do you adore God with your life? Does your life set Him on high? Are you an example to other believers? Do you mirror His attributes by doing justly, loving mercy, and walking humbly with Him as your God? Do you rejoice in the Lord always?

Do you hallow God's name by submitting your entire life to Him, giving everything to Him, even those besetting sins that you battle day and night? Do you surrender everything to God without murmuring, or are there parts of your life that you have not yet given to God? Do your actions coincide with your thoughts, your desires, and your words? Is your life like one large tapestry of obedience to God, of desiring to glorify Him, and of belonging not to yourself but to Him? Do you pray that the whole world might bow before the great hallowed name of God in reverence, praise, worship, honor, and humility?

How do you spend the Lord's Day? How do you spend the other six days? What do you do with your time? What do you read? Who are your closest friends? Does everything in your life speak one language, declaring, "Hallowed be Thy name?" Are you striving to hallow God's name in your family, your congregation, in the work place, at school? Does your life testify to the glory, beauty, personality, and holiness of God? If we realize how broad the scope of this petition is, we will be grateful that this petition is not a claim to have achieved perfection, but the humble prayer to grow in grace (Philippians 3:13–14): "Grant us, O God, rightly to know Thee. Grant that we may honor Thy holiness. Grant that we may order and direct our whole lives to this end. Grant that our thoughts, words, and actions may not blaspheme Thy Name, but honor and praise Thee."

The child of God has been delivered from the penalty and power of sin through union with his Savior, but not from sin's indwelling presence. From time to time, through weakness, we fall into sin. In so doing we cause the name of God to be blasphemed among unbelievers. That was true of David, the man after God's own heart. After David's adulterous affair with Bathsheba, the prophet Nathan said to the king, "By this deed thou hast given great occasion to the enemies of the LORD to blaspheme" (2 Samuel 12:14). An unbelieving world looks for just such occasions to justify its unbelief. The enemies of the gospel are "watching for our halting" (Jeremiah 20:10). We thus need to be on guard, maintaining a watch against all failures and inconsistencies in our walk of faith and manner of life.

In the past it was common for people who professed to be Christians to wear "WWJD" (What Would Jesus Do) bracelets as a kind of badge of their faith. I cringed at times at the behavior of some of these people. Professional athletes wore these bracelets as they played their sport on the Lord's Day. They professed to be a Christian and yet were blatant Sabbath breakers. How often a Christian profession is mingled with actions that are violations of God's law!

If we profess to be Christians, we are called to walk circumspectly in this world so that we do not give the world an opportunity to point fingers at our ungodly conduct and, ultimately, at our God. If we fall into sin, we must not despair of God's mercy nor continue in sin, for we have a covenant with a holy God. The psalmist who prayed that God would turn away the reproach he feared also prayed: "Hold Thou me up and I shall be safe" (Psalm 119:117). David prayed likewise, "keep back Thy servant from presumptuous sins; let them not have dominion over me" (Psalm 19:13). These are the prayers of one who fears God and hates sin.

To hallow God's name we must be conformed to the will of God. God's will is that His holiness be acknowledged, adored, and honored by us. It is the will of God ultimately to reveal His holiness and justice at the Judgment Day, so as to compel even the wicked to glorify Him and justify their own condemnation. So when we pray "Hallowed be Thy name," we identify with God's desire for His own glory. We submit ourselves to His name, His glory, and His perfections. When we pray "Hallowed be Thy name," we are praying, "Lord, grant us grace to be patient in adversity and thankful in prosperity. Grant us faith to trust in Thee as our faithful God and Father, being fully persuaded that nothing shall separate us from Thy love since we and all creatures are so in Thy hand, that without Thy will we cannot so much as move. So whatever befalls us, whatever becomes of us, whatever our future may be, let Thy name be hallowed and glorified in us, even if we must go through the deep ways of affliction and death. O Father in heaven, let Thy name be hallowed in all our sorrows." The profound depth of this petition "Hallowed be Thy name" requires us to honor God's name above our pleasures and our own will, and to bring our will into alignment with God's will for our lives.

Nothing can spiritually align God's people with God's will more than to begin their prayers by saying, "Lord, whatever Thou doest, and whatever I must encounter today or in the future, hallow Thy Name in me." By nature, it is impossible for us to align our will to God's, but it is not impossible for God to do this in us through the Mediator, our Lord Jesus Christ, who works in us by His Word and Spirit.

Christ can work it in us first of all because He Himself prayed, "O my Father, if it be possible, let this cup pass from Me; nevertheless not as I will, but as Thou wilt" (Matthew 26:39). He knows how hard it is for us as human beings to drink a cup of suffering. Jesus said to the Father, "If to hallow Thy name and do Thy will I must drink this cup, if I must endure a cruel trial of mocking and scourging, if they stretch Me out on the cross and pierce My hands and My feet, if I must be lifted up to die, if Thou must forsake Me while I descend into a pit of anguish and torment in utter darkness—heavenly Father, here I am. Thy name be hallowed. Thy name be glorified."

Christ hallowed God's name by submitting to God's will and laying down His life. His business was always to be about His Father's business and to glorify His Father's name. He can therefore work the same faith and attitude of heart in us poor sinners today. When we pray "Hallowed be Thy name," we unite our prayers with the earthly prayers of Christ, the heavenly intercession of Christ, and the inward intercession of the Holy Spirit for us. Nothing is more blessed than to pray, "Hallowed be Thy name," knowing that such is the will and power of God that this prayer shall truly and certainly be answered, above all that we could ask or think.

# Praying In Jesus' Name
## Steven J. Lawson

"Truly, truly, I say to you, he who believes in Me, the works that I do, he will do also; and greater works than these he will do because I go to the Father. Whatever you ask in My name, that will I do, so that the Father may be glorified in the Son. If you ask Me anything in My name, I will do it" (John 14:12–14, NASB).

At the height of the Protestant Reformation, Martin Luther, the great German reformer, once thundered, "Prayer is the mightiest of all weapons that created natures can wield." Here we learn the secret source of strength for this powerful figure in church history. With the demands of the sixteenth-century Reformation weighting heavily upon him, Luther further quipped, "I have so much to do today, I must spend three more hours this morning in prayer." Such was the pivotal role that prayer played in the life of this titanic figure.

Simply put, prayer is the infinite power of God committed to the hand of mere finite man. It *is* the closest that man can come to wielding divine omnipotence. Nothing can prevail against prayer, not even Satan and hell itself. Yet, tragically, prayer is often the most neglected of all Christian disciplines. And our lives and ministries suffer for it.

But, the fact is, there is a vital connection between our ministry involvements for the kingdom of God and praying, specifically, in Jesus' name. In other words, the latter is the God-ordained means by which the former becomes reality. God desires to perform greater works through us, and His stated channel by which He brings it to pass is our calling upon Him in prayer, in the name that is above every name, the name of Jesus Christ.

In John 14:12-14, Jesus Christ makes a staggering promise to every disciple. In His "Upper Room Discourse," having stated that He will be leaving them and returning to the Father, Jesus guaranteed His disciples that in His absence they would be empowered for the work of ministry. Specifically, Christ promises them "if you ask Me anything in My name, I will do it." Herein is the privilege and power of prayer that is afforded to each one of Christ's disciples. This assurance is the pledge of Christ Himself, to stand with His people in every walk of life in order to bring to bear all the limitless resources of heaven and earth to bear upon their lives and ministries.

### A Blank Check?

Many, unfortunately, have taken this divine promise to mean that they can ask for absolutely anything, and God is obligated to provide it. It is as if God has written them a pre-signed, blank check, such that they can fill in whatever amount is desired. Under such a scheme, God becomes nothing more than a mere cosmic genie in a bottle that when rubbed and the magical incantation, "in Jesus' name," is spoken, He will emerge to be their servant and grant their every wish.

But praying in Jesus' name is not a magic formula that, if simply repeated, will open Aladdin's lamp. This is why Jesus warned, "Do not use meaningless repetition as the Gentiles do" (Matthew 6:7). The mindless repetition of the mantra, "in Jesus' name" will not bring the answer to one's prayers. To pray in such a vain manner is to reduce this access to supernatural power to the level of mere religious superstition and empty lore.

In His model prayer in Matthew 6:9-15, Jesus never actually instructed His disciples that every prayer was to conclude with these words, "in Jesus' name." This phrase is to not simply be tacked on to the end as though it mystically gains one entrance into the treasures of heaven. There is certainly nothing wrong with concluding a prayer with these words. After all, these words are biblical. But when Jesus taught us to pray in His name, these words are a theological foundation, direction, and goal for our prayers, not a methodological technique.

In addition, those who suppose that praying "in Jesus' name" means you can ask for wealth and health fail to realize that it never worked for Jesus when He prayed. To the contrary, Christ died a horrible death at a young age, hanging naked upon a dreadful cross. Wealth certainly avoided Him. He had no place to lay His head. He had no money even to pay His taxes. He owned only one coat. Yet Jesus was a man of constant prayer. So, why did this not work for Him? To pray "in Jesus' name" must mean something else.

If the above mentioned is not what it means to pray in Jesus' name, then what does it mean? How are our Lord's words to be understood? What did He mean by what He said? The following are key distinctives that lead us into the proper meaning of these words.

**An Unlikely, Unimpressive Group**

In the final hours before the crucifixion of Jesus Christ, His disciples stood in dire need of encouragement. They had begun to grasp the words Christ had just spoken to them that they will not be going with Him, but will be remaining. In His absence, Jesus will be entrusting His entire ministry to them. Never has any band of men been charged with a greater assignment than this. In but a few days, they would be commissioned to reach the entire world with the gospel of the kingdom and to make disciples of all nations.

But consider who they were and what they were up against. They were hardly an impressive lot. They were not exactly the cream of the crop. They were unimposing and unorganized, uneducated and unlettered, uncouth and uncultured. They had virtually no resources—no buildings, no possessions, no clout, no programs, no marketing strategies, no advertisement, no financial backing, and no media outlets. They were on the outside looking in at the religious establishment of Israel. They were a ragtag collection of a common fisherman, a hated tax collector, and the rest were virtually anonymous.

All the disciples would have had was the despised message of a publicly-executed Jew. Their location was even worse. They began their ministry in the very city where Jesus had been crucified but days earlier. This was hardly an ideal spot for the first church plant. Further, this forsaken lot faced opposition of every kind. They faced the external attacks of Roman tyranny, Greek paganism, and Jewish legalism, to say nothing of Eastern mysticism and insipid Gnosticism. They suffered slander, ridicule, riot, police action, arrest, imprisonment, and even a martyr's death.

Yet, despite such overwhelming odds, by the end of the first century the Church had already extended down into Africa, as far south as Ethiopia. The Church, likewise, spread north into Asia Minor, where it thrived. Moreover, the Church spread east into continental Europe, as far as Rome, the capital city of the known world, where it established a beachhead in Caesar's own household.

How can this be explained? How could such an unimpressive group make such giant strides into three continents? In Jesus' absence, how did they carry out this imposing task? How did they overcome the imperial might of the Roman Empire? How did they survive in the face of the hardened, apostate Israel? How did they succeed?

## The Power of Prayer

The answer to these questions lies in what Jesus said to them in these verses in John 14:12-14. They would succeed, largely, in the power of prayer. Jesus instructed them that they were to pray to the Father in His name, asking Him to meet their needs, to carry out this God-appointed mission. In response to their prayers, Jesus guaranteed that He would provide for all their needs according to His sovereign authority. Jesus would build His church, convert their enemies, overturn their circumstances, and rout the forces of darkness. All this and more would be achieved through prayer in Jesus' name.

These verses contain the amazing promises that He made to His disciples. Here is the privilege of prayer that is afforded to all who believe in Him. This promise contains the pledge of Christ Himself to marshal all the resources of heaven and earth to bear upon our lives as needed.

## THE STAGGERING PROSPECT

But before Jesus would address the subject of prayer, He first made another astounding promise. Looking into the eyes of His disciples He said, "Truly, truly, I say to you, he who believes in Me, the works that I do, he will do also; and greater works than these he will do because I go to the Father" (verse 12). Everything that Jesus said is true, but some things rise to a higher level of importance. The words "Truly, truly, I say to you" elevates what He is saying to a state of critical significance. What will follow is what the disciples especially needed to hear.

**Greater Works Than Jesus**

Looking to the future, Jesus foretells, "he who believes in Me, the works that I do, he will do also" (verse 12). This is to say, these first followers of Christ would enter into the very works that Jesus had begun to do. At the heart of this assign-ment, these disciples would be preaching the very same message that He proclaimed. They would be announcing the very same truth concerning entrance into the kingdom of God. They would be calling sinners to repentance and urging those outside the kingdom to enter by saving faith in Him.

Yet Jesus made this extraordinary claim that their work would even exceed His work. He stated, "and greater works than these he will do because I go to the Father." Greater works? Can this be true? Certainly this could not mean greater in quality. How could they do anything better than the fully divine Son of God? Jesus performed everything perfectly without any blemish or flaw. His exposition of the Law was perfect. The motives of His heart were infinitely pure. The compassion He showed was untainted love.

How could the disciples possibly perform "greater works" than Jesus? The answer is, their works would be greater not in quality, but in quantity. The public ministry of Christ was short-lived, comprising little more than three years. But His disciples would minister for six more decades. Peter would preach for another thirty years, and John for another sixty years. In that extended period of time, they would collectively preach more messages than Christ. After all, there were eleven of them and only one of Him. The twelve disciples would preach far more sermons, numerically speaking, than did Christ by Himself.

In addition, these disciples would perform works of far greater extent. Jesus never saw more than a few hundred believe, but Peter witnessed 3,000 receive the gospel in his first sermon alone. Jesus never preached beyond Palestine, yet His followers would proclaim the gospel throughout the known world. Jesus had only a limited outreach to Gentiles, but the disciples, particularly Peter and later Paul, would spread the gospel to the Gentile world—all the way to Rome. In all, the multiplied thousands they reached far exceeded the mere hundreds that entered the kingdom during Christ's three years of preaching. In this sense, the greater works that would be performed by Christ's disciples were greater in both size and scope, in number and in territory.

### The Right Hand of God

What Jesus says next identifies the key to the disciple's success. They will prosper in ministry "because I go to the Father." His departure to the Father will enthrone Him at the right hand of the Majesty on high. This is the reason why the disciples would do greater things than Christ Himself. Simply put, Christ will more fully demonstrate His power from heaven than when He was on the earth for two obvious reasons. One, Jesus will send the Holy Spirit, who will empower them to fulfill the mission (John 14:16-20; 15:26; 16:8-15; Acts 1:8; 2:1-4), and, two, He will be the Mediator for their prayers to the Father. As He will explain in the next two verses, they pray in His name and, in turn, He will supply their every need to fulfill this extraordinary mission.

### THE STAGGERING PROMISE

In the next verse, Jesus now explains to His disciples the power of prayer. He emphatically states, "Whatever you ask in My name, that will I do." In these prolific words, there is no hesitancy on His part in answering their prayers. Neither is there any reluctance by Him. Jesus expresses that He is ready to answer their every request for His assistance to fulfill the high task to which they have been called.

### Whatever You Ask For

The word "whatever" makes this promise extraordinarily wide. This open-ended word indicates that they should pray for "whatever," whether it is for large or small things, spiritual or physical needs, personal or corporate requests. In other words, there is no restriction to the areas in which they should petition God. "Whatever" is necessary to carry out these greater works, God will supply. Further, the word, "ask," means to make a request of another person for something. It is to make appeal for something. It is to solicit another. In the case of prayer, it is making known to God our specific needs and requesting Him to meet those needs.

Regarding this need to ask God in prayer, Jesus had earlier taught: "Ask, and it will be given to you; seek, and you will find; knock, and it will be opened to you" (Matthew 7:7). There is an intended progression here from asking to seeking, and from seeking to knocking. A building intensity is represented here. Each of these verbs is in the present tense, meaning "keep on asking, be always seeking, do not stop knocking." In other words, make it a lifestyle of continually bringing your needs to God in prayer and asking Him to meet those needs. For the Scripture says: "With God all things are possible" (Matthew 19:26).

But too often Christians fail to actually ask God in prayer to address a matter in their lives. Instead they focus upon it and brood over it, often becoming stressed about it, even becoming discouraged under its heavy load. They fail to actually bring the matter to God in prayer. The Bible says: "You do not have because you do not ask" (James 4:2). Certainly, believers are un-willing to ask for God's grace and assistance. But clearly, Jesus instructs us and invites us to ask of Him.

### The Pledge of Sovereignty

In response, Jesus said, "that will I do." Jesus Christ claims that He will personally meet their requests. Our Lord Himself will be directly involved in supplying their needs. He will be the Source of all that the disciples will need. Moreover, there is no reluctance on the part of Christ to answer the prayers of His disciples. He wants them to know, in no uncertain terms, that He stands ready to meet their needs. He will continue to be ac-tively involved in their lives and ministries. When He says He will do it, He *will* actually do it. The fidelity of His words and the faithfulness of His Person are at stake. They will ask and He will answer. They will intercede and He will intervene.

## THE STAGGERING PREREQUISITE

Having encouraged the disciples that "whatever you ask," "that I will do," Jesus adds an all-important qualifier in the mid-dle of these two statements. He says that we must pray "in My name." This small, three-word, prepositional phrase is the key that unlocks the large door leading to answered prayers. If they will come to the Father in His name, the Father will answer and Jesus will provide. Everything hinges on praying in His name. But what does it mean to pray in Jesus' name?

### Access in Jesus' Name

First, *it means to have access to God in Jesus' name.* Praying in Jesus' name means to realize that we have no basis of acceptance before God apart from the Person and work of Jesus Christ. We cannot approach the throne of God apart from coming in the name of Jesus Christ. Jesus made this clear when He said, "I am the way and the truth and the life. No one comes to the Father but through Me" (John 14:6). When Jesus died upon the cross, the veil was torn in the temple, opening the way into the Holy of Holies (Matthew 27:51). This symbolized that Christ, by His death, opened direct and personal access to God for His people.

By His substitutionary death, Jesus opened up the only entrance whereby we may approach a holy God in heaven. The Bible says, "We have confidence to enter the holy place by the blood of Jesus, by a new and living way which He inaugurated for us through the veil, that is, His flesh." As a result, "let us draw near with a sincere heart in full assurance of faith" (Hebrews 10:19–22). It is only by means of Jesus Christ that we can come before the throne of grace. To come in Jesus' name is to acknowledge one's own spiritual poverty and utter unworthiness. Therefore, we approach God the Father on no other basis and in no other merit than that of our Lord Jesus Christ.

With this in mind, sometimes people ask, "When I pray, do I pray to the Father or do I pray to the Son? Do I pray to the Holy Spirit?" Paul clarifies this when he writes: "For through Him [Christ] we have our access in the Spirit to the Father" (Ephesians 2:18). Clearly, prayer is Trinitarian. We pray *to* the Father *through* the Son *in* the Spirit. Jesus had already taught this: "When you pray, pray like this. 'Our Father, who art in heaven, hallowed would be Thy name' " (Matthew 6:9). In prayer, His disciples are to approach God the Father through the Son, under the guidance of the Spirit, Who directs our minds and hearts in what we should pray.

## Agreement With His Name

Second, *it means to pray in agreement with God's character and will.* In the ancient world, a name meant the sum total of all that a person was. A name in the Bible, likewise, represented the whole of that person, the totality of who one was—his nature, character, and attributes. This means that when we pray, we do so in conformity with Jesus' character and His attributes. We pray according to what is consistent with His holiness, sovereignty, mercy, love, righteousness, immutability, truth, and all His other divine attributes. In our prayers we must then ask ourselves: Is what we are petitioning something that Jesus would endorse? Can Jesus subscribe to this prayer that is being offered to the Father by us? There is an affirmative to the prayers that are offered in Jesus' name.

To pray in Jesus' name thus means to ask for those things that are in agreement with His holy character and the sovereign will of God. Praying in His name expresses the alignment of one's desires and purposes with Christ. That is to say, our requests must be in agreement with the perfections of His divine being. We pray for that which is in keeping with His holy attributes. Simply put, our prayers must be consistent with the desires of our Lord. We are to pray for what He would pray. We are to prayerfully desire that which He desires. We are to seek what He seeks. We are to promote that which He has at heart. In prayer, His priorities must be our priorities. His passions must be our passions. His agenda must be our agenda.

To petition the Father in the name of Christ is to set aside our own will and bow to the perfect will of God. Many times we will pray, "If it is Your will, God, then may it be so." The will of God is that which is "good and acceptable and perfect" (Romans 12:2). We pray with such limited perspective. But God hears and answers with unlimited knowledge. God knows more than we know and is much wiser than we are. God knows what is best, and He has something far better for us. So we need to pray in accordance with His perfect character, His perfect attributes, and His perfect will. Nothing should be brought before the throne of God that is inconsistent with the perfect righteousness and holiness of God. We should never pray for that which is outside of His revealed will in Scripture. Instead, we must pray for those things that are consistent with His perfect character and will.

### Advancement of Jesus' Name

Third, *it means to pray for the advancement of Jesus' name*. To pray in Jesus' name means to pray for those things that have as their ultimate target the spreading of the name of Jesus Christ. It means to pray for those things that cause the name of Jesus Christ to be believed upon, embraced, and cherished. This is the chief purpose of God in the world, the spreading of the fame of Christ's name. This means that our requests are to focus upon the purposes of His kingdom. This is what Jesus meant when He taught His disciples to pray, "Your kingdom come. Your will be done, on earth as it is in heaven" (Matthew 6:10). Here is the chief thrust behind asking God for anything. It is prayer aimed at carrying forward the work Jesus did. It is to advance the name of Christ throughout the world. This is the prayer that He Himself will answer.

In John 15:16 Jesus said, "You did not choose Me, but I chose you, and appointed you that you should go and bear fruit and that your fruit should remain so that whatever you ask of the Father in My name He may give it to you." This fruit is fruit that comes from our labor for Him as we witness for Him, as we share the gospel, as we serve in His name to advance the kingdom. Praying in the name of Jesus is directly connected with

going and bearing fruit, and asking that your fruit would remain. He is talking about your ministry. He is talking about
your service for Him. He is talking about the advancement of
the kingdom of God through your life, whatever it is God has
put you here upon this earth to do to play your part and to carry
out your role in the advancement of God's kingdom. As you
pray, Jesus will open doors, He will supply needs, and He will
supply encouragement and resources, whatever is necessary for
you to do greater works in His name.

This is precisely what happened on the Day of Pentecost:
"The Lord was adding to their number day by day those who
were being saved" (Acts 2:47). Three thousand souls were saved.
It happened with Peter. And that was the first fulfillment of this
promise that you will do greater works than Christ, greater in
extent, greater in far-reaching impact as you pray in His name.
Consider again where Peter was prior to his preaching. He was
in the Upper Room praying. Jesus was not there, but, having
ascended to heaven ten days earlier, He was seated at the right
hand of God the Father. Peter and the early believers were praying in Jesus' name. What was the first answer to their prayers? It
is what occurred on the Day of Pentecost in the great harvest of
many souls. Further, the same took place in varying degrees in
Jerusalem, in Judea, in Samaria, and in the uttermost regions of
the earth.

## THE STAGGERING PURPOSE

Overall, there must be one chief motive and overarching
purpose in prayer, and that is *Soli Deo Gloria*—for the glory of
God alone. The believer's prayer should always be, as Jesus says,
"that the Father may be glorified in the Son." Many people
wrongly assume that prayer is fundamentally about getting

something from God. But the fact is, prayer is actually a means by which God receives something from us. In other words, through our prayers God is, first and foremost, to receive ascribed glory. All prayer is, therefore, to be for the passionate pursuit of this highest purpose, namely the honor due His name.

### Glorifying the Father

Prayer, Jesus taught, is "that the Father may be glorified." In other words, it is not to be self-focused, but God-exalting. Making petition of God must be theo-centric, that is, God-centered. The highest apex of our prayers must be pointed toward the magnification of His name, the elevation of His name, and the advancement of His kingdom. Prayer is not chiefly getting something from God for ourselves. Rather, it is actually a means by which God receives something from us. What He desires from us is glory given to His name. The chief goal in prayer is not the fulfilling of our own well-being. Rather, it is for the glorification of the name of God.

When Jesus taught us to pray, He stated that the highest aim must be the exaltation of God's glory. We are to commence and conclude prayer with prizing the glory of God. Jesus said we should begin our prayers with this supreme focus: "Our Father who is in heaven, hallowed be Your name" (Matthew 6:9). Further, this pursuit of God's glory is how Jesus began His own prayers. Jesus started one prayer, "I praise You, Father, Lord of heaven and earth" (Matthew 11:25). Another time Jesus prayed, "Father, glorify Your name" (John 12:28). The night before His crucifixion Jesus prayed, "Father, the hour has come; glorify Your Son, that the Son may glorify You" (John 17:1). To be sure, the end of all things in prayer, as John Calvin once said, is the sanctification of God.

### A Glory in the Son

As Jesus instructed His disciples in glorifying God in prayer, He stated that it must be "in the Son." In other words, the Father is supremely glorified in and through His Son. To be specific, the Father receives glory through the Son's perfect obedience. During Christ's ministry on earth, the Son's consistent aim was to bring glory to His Father. Nowhere is this greater evidenced than in Jesus' purposing to complete His mission by going to the cross, the means by which the Father would be most glorified in the Son. All that the Father would grant in response to their prayers, which focus upon the glory of the Son, will be the means of great glory being brought to Him.

In addition, the Father is uniquely honored when the Son is magnified. This is precisely what Paul taught: "and that every tongue will confess that Jesus Christ is Lord, to the glory of God the Father" (Philippians 2:11). The purpose of Christ's exaltation is God's glorification. The two are inseparably connected together. The disciples should pray for the Father to be honored in and through the mediation of the Son. Jesus enables His people to do "greater works" in order that the Father may be glorified in the Son. This is the result of praying in Jesus' name. To pray in Jesus' name promotes the glory of the Father in the Son. This is the highest end of all things and achieves the greatest good.

## THE STAGGERING POWER

As Jesus brings this cluster of promises to conclusion, He intentionally reasserts what He has just stated to His disciples. Jesus says once again, "If you ask Me anything in My name, I will do it" (John 14:14). This is not, as Calvin says, a useless repetition. This verse repeats what Jesus previously stated to give emphasis to the promise and assurance to the disciples. It is as if our Lord knew how difficult it would be for them to believe the power afforded to them in prayer. Consequently, Jesus tells them one more time, most emphatically, that if they will ask anything in His name He will do it.

### The Reinforcement of the Promise

Jesus begins this reinforcement by stating the condition, "If you ask Me anything in My name." Many believers will fail to ask because the promise seems to be too abundant, limitless, and free. But this condition must be met. All disciples must come before the Lord and purposely ask Him to meet their needs. This is a spiritual discipline that requires the exercise of faith and the intentionality of the will. Here, Jesus instructs believers to ask Him, as opposed to the Father. This again teaches the Oneness of the Godhead and the closeness of their operations. To trust the Son is to trust the Father and vice versa.

Again, disciples are to ask in the name of Christ. There is no other way for their prayers to be answered. There is no alternate approach before the Father or the Son. All prayers must be by the access of the name of Christ, that is, by faith in the sufficiency of His perfect atonement for our sins. Further, the prayers of believers will only be answered to the extent that they are in alignment with the character of Christ and the sovereign will of the Father. Moreover, their prayers will come to pass as they advance the kingdom and purposes of Jesus Christ here upon the earth. This is the prerequisite that must be met. As Jesus repeats this, it is to leave an indelible impression upon the minds of His disciples.

### The Glorious Answer

Once again, Jesus emphatically promises, "I will do it." Few words could have been more encouraging to these disciples at this time than to have heard this positive assertion. It is as though Jesus is deliberately etching this promise into their minds. To the extent that their prayers have been to promote the glory of the Son, the Son will ensure that their requests will be completely met. Certainly, God's timing will not always be that of His disciples. Many times they must wait for the answer to come. And surely God's wisdom will often dictate that the prayers be answered in ways other than they have asked. Sometimes, in God's inscrutable wisdom, the answer is even withheld. But such a negative, in reality, is a positive because He alone knows what is best for His own. When His disciples ask in faith, He *will* surely do it, for His glory and for their good.

We, too, need to have these words repeated to our minds and reinforced in our hearts. Likewise, we are slow to believe in the staggering power of this promise. How often do we doubt the power of God in prayer? How often do we fail to pray because this promise is seemingly too good? Our lack of prayer indicates that we fail to truly believe what Christ is saying in these words. If we truly believed in this promise of prayer, we would pray more.

### Bringing Awesome Requests

As we look inside these few verses, we certainly see that God greatly desires for His people to pray. Herein, we are encouraged to pray. We are told that if we will pray, the Father will hear and that there are many things that He will give to us in order to carry out His will. So, as we come to the Lord in prayer, may we all be encouraged to move out the boundaries for what we are praying, to push beyond mere trifling requests and to ask of

Him great and awesome things that only He can do. The truth is, we probably have asked for too little from God, certainly not too much.

A woman once approached the London expositor G. Campbell Morgan after a church service asking, "May I pray for small things in my life? Or only large things?" Morgan, with keen insight, answered, "Madam, there is nothing big in your life. Everything is small when compared to God." Morgan made his point. We should bring the request for all our needs to God in prayer. There is nothing too small, or seemingly insignificant, for us to petition God. And there is certainly no shortage of His ability and resources to answer our requests.

Let us come with confidence before His throne of grace and ask in the name of Jesus that He perform greater works in and through our lives so that the Father may be glorified in the Son.

# Seeking God's Will in Prayer
## W. Robert Godfrey
### 2 Kings 18:29-45; 19:15-19; 19:35-20:6

Hezekiah was a most remarkable king. After David, he was perhaps the most righteous and faithful king that reigned in Judah. He did remarkable acts of service to the Lord, particularly protecting the Lord's worship and purifying it. But Hezekiah was also a great man of prayer, and in the prayer of Hezekiah we can see something of a model for us as to what prayer to the true and living God should be.

Hezekiah is presented to us in our text through two prayers that he offers to the Lord. The first prayer is that God might be glorified in the defeat of Sennacherib's army. Such is rather easy to understand, and seems to fit in well with our general understanding of prayer and our relationship to God in prayer. But the second prayer, when Hezekiah falls sick, is not so easy to understand. 2 Kings 20:3 records that brief second prayer of Hezekiah:

> Remember now, O Lord, I beseech Thee, how I have walked before Thee in truth and with a whole heart, and have done what is good in Thy sight.

How many of us would be likely to pray a prayer like that? "O Lord, I've loved the truth. I've served you wholeheartedly and I've done what is good. So you should be good to me." How are we to understand this prayer? What does this prayer really mean? At least one commentator suggests that it is not really a godly prayer at all. The commentator says that this prayer is "characterized by its self-centeredness, not its faith." But is that really a valid way of assessing this prayer? After all, the Lord answers this prayer. We are told that the Lord hears this prayer and heals Hezekiah. So it does not seem that the Lord treats this prayer as somehow selfish or self-centered or sinful. If this is a godly prayer, what can we learn from it? What can we learn from this, and the experience of Hezekiah to help us to be similarly faithful praying people?

Just so there will not be too many expectations for this article at the outset, let me say that we are not going to learn that whenever the people of God fall sick they can pray and be healed. That is not at all what Hezekiah's prayer teaches us. But it does teach us some very crucial things about how we are to pray, and what we are to expect from the Lord as we pray.

### The Problems of Hezekiah

In order to profit from this prayer we have to look at exactly what the problem is that Hezekiah faces that leads him to pray as he does. What are the problems in Hezekiah's life? The first problem is the obvious one: he's sick! He's very sick. He is miserably sick. If we had read a little further in chapter 20, we would have seen that the prophet Isaiah is told to make a paste out of figs to rub on what appear to be ulcers on his skin. This is really a miserable, wasting kind of disease that has struck a relatively young Hezekiah. Hezekiah is 39. Yet he is sick with a sickness unto death. He has only been on the throne 14 years.

As if that sickness were not enough, he has a prophet come to him and say to him that he had better set his affairs in order, for he will surely die. This is not the kind of pastoral visit that most of us look for when we are sick. Here the great prophet Isaiah comes with this word of doom—no word or encouragement, no word of hope, simply this word of doom.

And yet as we look more closely at this story of Hezekiah, we begin to see that his sickness is only a part and expression of a deeper problem that he wrestles with in prayer. It is not just his sickness that worries Hezekiah and drives him to prayer. At a deeper level, he is worried about what this sickness says about the faithfulness and reliability of God and His promises. One of the things we see as we study this story of Hezekiah is that he was a man who knew the Bible and its promises intimately. His mind and heart were filled with the Scriptures and, as he meditated on the Scriptures, he knew that the Lord had made certain promises to Israel. He knew that when the Lord had set Israel apart to be a showcase for His redeeming work among the nations, God had made a promise to Israel, a promise expressed, for example, in Deuteronomy 4:39–40:

> Know therefore today, and take it to your heart, that the Lord, he is God in heaven above and on the earth below; there is no other. So you shall keep his statutes and his commandments which I am giving you today, that it may go well with you and your children after you, and that you may prolong your days on the land which the Lord your God is giving you for all time.

The Lord had promised length of days to His people in Israel. That was part of the unique blessing that the Lord was going to manifest among those old covenant people. He was going to show to the world that He was the Lord of life and display that truth in His people. Israel among the nations would have that unique experience to show the peoples of the world that Israel served a life-giving God.

Hezekiah, however, finds his life threatened. Hezekiah, only 14 years on the throne, only 39 years of age, is facing death and he goes to the Lord. He wrestles with the Lord about this question: "How can this be? How can this be in accord with Your promise to give life? I have been one of your most faithful kings and yet my reign is a rather short one. How does this relate to Your promise? How does this manifest Your glory?"

Beyond the general promise of life, Hezekiah sees a special reason for life in his situation. Hezekiah thinks specifically of the comparison between himself and Sennacherib. Think with Hezekiah about Sennacherib. Sennacherib had invaded Judah and he had come as a very well-informed invader. Somebody had studied the Judeans for Sennacherib and had given him very good information as to what kind of people they were, what their culture was, and what their religion was. He had heard that they had this strange monotheistic religion. So Sennacherib comes into Judah and says, "Jehovah sent me." His spies must have told him that this might be meaningful to the people, and so he comes, presuming to come in the name of the Lord. He appears to have been informed that the God of Israel was the God who had promised His people a land flowing with milk and honey, a land of peace and prosperity. So Sennacherib comes saying, "I will give you peace. I will give you prosperity. I will give the fruit of your figs and vines, or, if I don't let you stay in this land with your figs and vines, I will take you to a land just like yours, just as good as yours. You will have peace and you will have prosperity there." Sennacherib says, "Don't go to war with me. Don't choose death. Choose life. I'm the one who can give you life. Don't put any trust in those promises of Hezekiah that the Lord will deliver you, for none of the gods of the nations can stand before me." So Sennacherib comes as if he were God. Sennacherib comes as if he were Messiah, as if he were the Christ bearing these promises of life and peace and prosperity. He claims to come in the name of the Lord to the people of God. In reality he exalts himself against the Lord and against His Word and against His promises. Sennacherib claims to be able to stand and conquer all the peoples and all the gods, including Jehovah. He comes as the proud blasphemer pretending to be the Lord's Messiah.

Against that pride and blasphemy, Hezekiah prays in his first prayer: "Now, O Lord, display before the nations Your glory. Now, O Lord, show that You are the true and living God, the only true and living God, and cast down this blasphemer before the nations so that all men may see that his pride is brought to naught and that You are exalted." And that, of course, is exactly what the Lord does. The Lord does strike down the blasphemer in the most dramatic way. His troops are decimated in one night. Sennacherib is forced to retreat to his capital, and even there he is not safe. Even in his temple and in the bosom of his family, he is not safe. His own sons rise up against him and strike him down in the temple of his god and he is destroyed. As Hezekiah reflects on the destruction of Sennacherib, he thinks, "Lord, if it is right that the faithless Sennacherib be struck down and die so that Your glory might be revealed among the nations, then it cannot be right that I should die in my youth when I have been good and faithful." You see how intense that problem is for Hezekiah. It is not right that the good and faithful anointed king of God's people should suffer the same fate as Sennacherib, the wicked monster who raised himself against God and His people. How can the glory of God be displayed in that?

As if these were not enough problems, there appears to be one more. It seems that Hezekiah at this point in his life has no son, no heir. We read that when the Lord healed Hezekiah, his life was extended by 15 years. Then we read that when Hezekiah died, his son Manassah came to the throne at age 12. So it appears that at this point, where Hezekiah is threatened with

death, he has no son to sit on David's throne. There is no son
to continue David's line. Therefore, the very line of Messiah is
threatened in this illness and this sentence of death that has
come upon Hezekiah. So out of all that, he turns to the Lord in
prayer. We have to keep the depth and complexity of Hezekiah's
problems in mind if we are to understand his prayer.

### The Prayer of Hezekiah

The first thing we notice about Hezekiah's second prayer is
that the very fact that he prays is a remarkable sign of the faithfulness of Hezekiah. Think how desperate his situation is. He
feels sick unto death. He has had the prophetic word that he is
going to die. How would you have reacted? I suspect that for
many of us there would be a tendency not to pray, but to be very
angry, or simply to be in a state of numb despair. "OK, I'm going to die; what's the point of anything? I'll just roll over and
die." But that is not Hezekiah's attitude. In his prayer we see the
man of faith, the man of God, revealed to us. In the midst of his
sickness, in the midst of this terrible situation that he confronts,
in the midst of distress about as serious as anyone can face, he is
a man of prayer. Here is an expression of the very heart of faith,
that in distress it turns to God, not away from God. In facing
problems, faith seeks help in God. It does not doubt God's
presence or despair of His goodness.

Hezekiah's prayer flows from a mind filled with Scripture. I
believe that he had in mind a psalm of David, Psalm 34. Let me
post some verses out of Psalm 34 to show how well they fit with
the situation of Hezekiah, and how knowing these promises
would have encouraged the man of faith to turn to God in
prayer:

> I sought the Lord and He answered me, and delivered me from all my fears (v. 4). This poor man cried and the Lord heard him and saved him out all his troubles (v. 6). Who is the man who desires life and loves length of days that he may see good? Keep your tongue from evil, and your lips from speaking deceit. Depart from evil and seek peace and pursue it. The eyes of the Lord are toward the righteous, and His ears are open to their cry. The face of the Lord is against evildoers to cut off their memory from the earth. They cry and the Lord hears, and delivers them out all their troubles. The Lord is near to the brokenhearted, and saves those who are crushed in spirit. Many are the afflictions of the righteous; but the Lord delivers him out them all (v. 12-19).

Here are the kinds of promises of the Word of God that encourage Hezekiah. The Lord has promised to hear the righteous. The Lord has promised to deliver the righteous. So Hezekiah turns to the Lord in prayer and says, "Lord, I have been faithful. I have kept Your covenant. I have been one who has sought to walk in Your ways."

Was Hezekiah saying that he was perfect? No! It is clear from Scripture that Hezekiah does not claim to be perfect. In Isaiah 38:17 we read another prayer of Hezekiah. There he prays: "It is Thou who hast kept my soul from the pit of nothingness, for Thou hast cast all my sins behind Thy back."

Hezekiah knew he was a sinner. Hezekiah knew that, left to himself, there was no good thing in him. But Hezekiah also knew that he had been redeemed by the grace of God, that he had been forgiven and renewed by the grace of God, that he had been made a part of God's covenant family. He knew that in the covenant family, by the grace of God he was a covenant keeper. When he turns to the Lord and says, "I have loved Your truth. I have walked in Your covenant. I have devoted myself to You," he is saying, "I have not been a covenant breaker like Sennacherib. I have not blasphemed against You. I have sought in all my life to serve You. So, Lord, be merciful to me. Lord, show me Your grace and Your favor. Lord, show me Your goodness in prolonging my life." Hezekiah prays very much in the spirit of Psalm 26:1–6.

We know that the only one who is truly righteous and the only one who keeps God's law and covenant is Jesus, the Messiah. And so we understand something about the covenant of grace even more deeply and more fully than Hezekiah did. When we pray, we are careful to come to God only in Jesus' name. We come in the name of the one who is truly righteous, the one who perfectly kept God's covenant in every way. Yet, like Hezekiah, those of us in Jesus Christ can come to God saying, "I am a covenant keeper. I am not perfect, but out of the intention of my heart, renewed by Your grace, I am striving to live for You, to serve You. I am Your child. I am part of Your covenant. O Lord, show me Your mercy; show me Your goodness."

When Hezekiah prays as a covenant-keeper for healing, he is not praying selfishly and self-centeredly for himself. He is not saying, "O Lord, I have been good, so You owe me something."

Rather, Hezekiah is reasoning with the Lord in prayer at a very profound level. He is really saying to the Lord, "You are the giver of life. You are the one who has always supplied Your people with life and health and strength. You are the one who can even raise one up from his deathbed, so that in the third day he may go into your temple and glorify you. You are the one, O Lord, who grants life to Your people. You are the one who raises the dead. To display your righteousness before the nations, as you have slain the wicked Sennacherib, so raise up the covenant-keeping Hezekiah that You might be glorified." At the heart of the second prayer of Hezekiah is the same prayer for God's glory that we saw in the first prayer of Hezekiah. He is not praying selfishly. He is not praying self-centeredly. He is praying for God's glory, for God's purpose to be fulfilled, for God's kingdom to come.

You see, such prayers should guide and direct our praying. I fear that our praying often runs the risk of degenerating into a kind of shopping list. "O Lord, I'd like A, then I'd like B, then I'd like C, and then I'd like D." It is like children drawing up a Christmas list. These are the things we'd like. To a point that is legitimate, but what Hezekiah challenges us to do in our prayers is to go a further step and reason with the Lord, to tell Him *why* we desire the things for which we ask.

How might it change our prayers if every time we offered a prayer to the Lord, we explained to Him how that particular request would advance the glory of His kingdom? Imagine a prayer meeting in which someone asks prayer for Aunt Bessie's broken leg. What if the leader of the meeting then said, "Why should we pray for Aunt Bessie's broken leg?" We might be shocked at first by such a question. But the question would encourage us to seek God-glorifying reasons for the requests we make to God. Perhaps if our prayers were focused on what advances God's glory, we would rearrange our priorities in prayer. Maybe we would begin to have prayers that were more spiritually directed to the great issues of God's kingdom. We are called to seek first the kingdom of God and His righteousness.

If we reason with God in prayer we will pray for His glory, and in the end we will pray that His will may be done. "Thy will be done" is always the pinnacle of prayer. It is not the first element of our prayer, as if in some Stoic fashion, having no feelings or emotions, we say "Thy will be done." No, we wrestle with the Lord in prayer; we present our petitions to the Lord in prayer; we try to reason with God to advance His glory. Then, when His glory has become our greatest concern, we can say, "Thy will be done." Then we understand that His will glorifies Himself best. When we say "Thy will be done," we are speaking as child to father, a father in whom we have utter confidence to do what is good and wise and right. Therefore, after we have opened our hearts to God as Hezekiah opened his heart, and as David so often does in the Psalms, we can at last turn it over to God and say, "Father, I love You and I trust You and I know that You are wiser in glorifying Yourself than I am. Therefore, Your will be done." Implicit in Hezekiah's prayer is this same sentiment: "It seems good to me, O Lord, that I should be raised from this sickness; but whether I get well or not, glorify Yourself, O Lord, and Your will be done." That is the kind of prayer that we are called upon to offer as we follow in the footsteps of Hezekiah.

The Lord shows His blessing upon Hezekiah by healing him, by raising him up, by uniting him in the fellowship of worship in His temple and by granting him 15 more years of life, and by giving him a son, and by delivering Jerusalem from the hand of the Assyrians. The Lord surely did glorify Himself in answering Hezekiah's prayer.

The Lord calls us then to pray seeking His glory. To pray person to person, to pray opening our hearts, to pray pouring out the deep desires of our hearts, our frustrations as well as our joys, but then to reason with God and with ourselves so that we too might be changed in prayer. We are to pray that God might be glorified and that His will might be done.

If we are to pray that way effectively, we need to do as Hezekiah did and fill our minds and hearts with the Word of God. Hezekiah's prayer flows out of his profound knowledge of God's purpose and the ways in which God glorifies Himself. Hezekiah's mind was clearly filled with the Psalms, and ours should be too. That is why it is so important that we sing the Psalms. We need those rich and deep roots of piety out of God's own Word to fill our hearts so that we might glorify Him. Sing Psalm 30 and unite with David (and Hezekiah) in celebrating the deliverance of the Lord.

May God encourage us to reason with Him in prayer to seek His own glory and to glory in His will.

# Prayer and the Sovereignty of God

## Richard D. Phillips

"For this reason, because I have heard of your faith in the Lord Jesus and your love toward all the saints, I do not cease to give thanks for you, remembering you in my prayers." Ephesians 1:15–16 (ESV)

A few years ago an interstate bridge collapsed in Minneapolis, taking the lives of more than a dozen people. Two large evangelical churches in Minneapolis responded to the tragedy, but explained it in entirely different ways. John Piper, whose church is located less than a mile from the bridge collapse, wrote a blog article on the night of the tragedy affirming that God was sovereign over the bridge collapse, seeing in it a call for sinners to repent.[1] Greg Boyd, the other pastor, responded to Piper's piece by publicly rejecting God's sovereignty over tragedies of this kind. Piper argued that the holy, good, and loving God is sovereign even over these events; they happen in accordance with His will. Boyd retorted that God could not be sovereign over such tragedies, or else He would not be holy, loving, and good. According to Boyd, tragedies of this kind happen because God is not sovereign over all things. "I suggest it's far more biblical, and far more rational," he wrote, "to simply say that in

---

[1] John Piper, "Putting My Daughter to Bed Two Hours after the Bridge Collapsed," accessed on-line August 2007 at: http://www.desiringgod.org/blog /posts/putting-my-daughter-to-bed-two-hours-after-the-bridge-collapsed.

that in a fallen, oppressed world, bridges sometimes collapse—and leave it at that."[2]

Boyd represents a theological movement known as "Open Theism," which maintains that God is neither omniscient over the future nor sovereign over the present. Another Open Theist, Roger Olson, responded to the bridge collapse by summarizing their overall view: "God is limited. . . .God limits Himself so that much of what happens in the world is due to human finitude and fallenness." He asked, "What if God wishes that things could be otherwise and someday will make all things perfect?" Olson then asserts, "That seems more like the God of the Bible than the all-determining deity of Calvinism."[3]

One of the aims of Open Theism is to give pastoral help to people who are angry with God for letting bad things happen. They want people not to be discouraged in their prayers by thinking that God doesn't care or that God wills things that seem bad to us. Instead, God cares greatly, they say, but He simply is not in control of all things. Olson explains: "In this world, because of our ignorance and sinfulness, really bad things sometimes happen and people do really evil and wicked things. Not because God secretly plans and prods them, but because God has said to fallen, sinful people, 'OK, not my will then, but thine be done ~ for now.'" Under this view, we should pray because God needs us to inform Him and help Him to make things better. Olson has God telling us, "Sometimes I can intervene to stop innocent suffering when people pray; that's one of

---

[2] Greg Boyd, "Why the I-35 Bridge Collapsed," accessed on-line August 9, 2007 available from http://gregboyd.blogspot.com/2007/08/why-35w-bridge-collapsed.html.

[3] Roger Olson, "Calvinistic View of Bridge Collapse Distorts God's Character," accessed August 27, 2007 online at http://www.baylor.edu/lariat/news.

My self-limitations. I don't want to do it all Myself; I want your involvement and partnership in making this a better world."[4]

The contrasting responses to the Minneapolis bridge collapse show us the importance of the question of God's sovereignty to the way we think as Christians, and especially to our understanding of prayer. It is not the purpose of this chapter to debate the matter of divine sovereignty and predestination, but rather to begin by affirming Jesus' teaching that not even a sparrow falls to the ground apart from the Father's will (Matthew 10:29). Our concern will instead be to address the relationship of God's sovereignty to the important subject of prayer. For some, the sovereignty of God seems to rule out the place of prayer altogether. Others struggle to understand the relationship between human responsibility—including our obligation to pray—and the Bible's teaching of God's sovereignty over all things and events. Taking Paul's prayer in Ephesians 1:15-21 as a starting place, we will seek to answer these questions and show that, according to Scripture, the sovereignty of God is in fact the greatest encouragement to prayer.

### If God Is Sovereign, Why Pray?

Do prayer and the sovereignty of God go together? If God is sovereign in all things, if God has ordained everything in advance according to His predetermined plan, then is there any point to praying? Why should we tell God our needs and cry to Him from our hearts if He knows all things in advance? For some, these and similar questions call the whole matter of God's sovereignty into question. "We know God wants us to pray," they argue, "and yet the idea of a sovereign, predestinating God seems incompatible with prayer."

---

[4] Ibid.

One way to realize that prayer must be compatible with God's sovereignty is to consider the example of the Apostle Paul. Throughout his many letters, Paul repeatedly and deliberately emphasized God's sovereignty. Ephesians chapter 1 especially concentrates Paul's teaching on this theme. In Ephesians 1:4, Paul says that God "chose us. . .before the foundation of the world." Verse 5 adds that He predestined us for adoption into His family. Verse 11 teaches that we were made heirs, "having been predestined according to the purpose of Him who works all things according to the counsel of His will." It is hard to imagine what stronger terminology Paul could possibly use to convey the idea that we are saved by God's sovereign grace. Indeed, Paul does not limit God's sovereignty to the sphere of salvation, but says in Acts 17:26 that "[God] made from one man every nation of mankind to live on all the face of the earth, having determined allotted periods and the boundaries of their dwelling place." God's sovereignty is unrestrained in Paul's thinking, but is unequivocal and total.

This emphasis on divine sovereignty raises questions about prayer. Did Paul's belief in God's complete sovereignty cause him to lose interest in prayer? Because God is in control, did Paul think little of the Christian's activity and responsibility? If, as many say, prayer and the sovereignty of God are incompatible, we should expect to see this play out in Paul's example more than in any other, with a de-emphasis on prayer to balance his emphasis on God's sovereign control. In fact, however, Paul's writings are noted not only for his teaching of God's sovereignty, but also for his highlighting of prayer. Paul was himself eminent as a man of prayer. Not only Ephesians, but all his letters overflow with prayer like flowers blossoming in a garden. Paul did not hesitate to ask his readers to pray for him (see Ephesians 6:19). Furthermore, Paul often prayed with direct reference to God's sovereignty. In 2 Thessalonians 2:13 he wrote: "We ought always to give thanks to God for you, brothers beloved by the Lord, because God chose you as the first fruits to be saved."

We are confronted, then, with this situation: The apostle most noted for teaching the highest view of God's total sovereignty was not thereby discouraged from praying, just as his belief in predestination did not lessen his zeal for evangelistic outreach and preaching. Instead, while strongly emphasizing God's sovereign election, Paul was singular in zeal for evangelism and prayer. C. Samuel Storms is surely right when he concludes: "That Paul should speak with perfect ease of both sovereign election and prayer. . .requires that we view them as theologically (and logically) compatible. Divine sovereignty does not preempt prayer, nor does prayer render God's choice contingent."[5]

We will find the same situation if we turn to the greater example of our Lord Jesus Christ. Think, for instance, of Jesus' prediction of Peter's denial. "I tell you, Peter," He said, "the rooster will not crow this day until you deny three times that you know Me" (Luke 22:34). Jesus' belief in divine sovereignty and foreknowledge is shown by His advance certainty of minute details such as the number of Peter's denials and the rooster's crowing. Jesus also knew that Peter would repent and be restored. Yet none of this sovereign foreknowledge deterred him from prayer. Jesus said to Peter, "Simon, Simon. . .I have prayed for you that your faith may not fail" (Luke 22:31–32).

---

[5] C. Samuel Storms, "Prayer and Evangelism under God's Sovereignty" in *Still Sovereign: Contemporary Perspectives on Election, Foreknowledge, and Grace*, ed. Thomas R. Schreiner & Bruce A. Ware (Grand Rapids: Baker, 1995), 316.

### God's Sovereignty as the Reason for Prayer

These examples give us sufficient reason to view prayer and God's sovereignty as fully compatible. Paul's prayer at the conclusion of Ephesians 1 gives us particularly keen insight into the relationship between the two. Ephesians 1:15–23 specifically tells us three things about prayer and the sovereignty of God. It says that because God is sovereign we have every reason to pray, we have every need to pray, and we have every encouragement to pray.

First is God's sovereignty as *a reason for prayer*. This is Paul's explicit statement in verses 15 and 16: "*For this reason*, because I have heard of your faith in the Lord Jesus and your love toward all the saints, I do not cease to give thanks for you, remembering you in my prayers." "For this reason" looks back on all that Paul had just taught, namely God's sovereign grace in Christ. It is in light of this that it occurs to him to pray for his readers. He thinks of them, recalls their faith and love, and, reflecting on God's sovereignty, he exclaims, "I have not stopped giving thanks for you."

So, if God is sovereign, why should we pray? First and foremost we pray to thank Him for the blessings of His sovereign grace. This is a vital reason for our prayer, to thank God for what He has done in our lives, knowing it is all of Him, and also for what He has done for others. Indeed, this recalls Paul's beginning to the whole letter: "Blessed be the God and Father of our Lord Jesus Christ, who has blessed us in Christ with every spiritual blessing in the heavenly places" (Ephesians 1:3). That is what he does in prayer: He praises and thanks God for all that He has done for us in Christ.

It is precisely because God is sovereign, because the salvation of these people came from His pure choice, that God alone is praised for their salvation. Were salvation not based on God's sovereignty, but at least in part on our supposedly free wills, then the praise would not all go to God. But Paul does not praise and thank the Ephesians for their faith and love, nor does he credit their pastors or even himself. Since God's sovereign grace is the cause of their salvation, all the praise and thanks goes to Him—and therefore Paul has a reason to pray to God.

Many people today reject Paul's doctrine of God's sovereignty, and one result is a diminishing emphasis on prayer in our churches. Towards the end of his ministry James Montgomery Boice began to notice that in so many of the churches he visited less and less time in corporate worship was being given to prayer. What prayer there was was tacked onto the service and dealt almost exclusively with requests for people who were sick and other needs. Christians were not reflecting on God's attributes or God's works in their prayers, nor were they praising or thanking Him. Reflecting on the great Reformation theme of *Soli Deo Gloria*—to God alone be the glory—Boice wrote this about those who deny God's sovereignty: "They want to glorify God. . .but they cannot say 'to God *alone* be glory,' because they insist on mixing human will power or ability with. . .gospel grace."[6]

As long as we believe that salvation results from man's sovereignty, from human choice and will and decision, denying the Bible's teaching that man contributes only his sin, and that God saves us by His sovereign, almighty grace alone, we will continue to focus on what we are doing and ought to do, neglecting prayer and the giving of praise and thanks to God. If ultimately it is human will that decides salvation, then we will appeal to humans and seek to please them instead of God. In contrast to

---

[6] James M. Boice, *Whatever Happened to the Gospel of Grace?* (Wheaton, Ill.: Crossway, 2001), 167. See also p. 178.

the man-centered spirit of our age, Paul's grand view of God's sovereignty supplies a compelling reason to pray, especially to give praise and thanks to God for His grace.

### God's Sovereignty and the Need for Prayer

God's sovereignty also provides *the need for prayer*. Paul asks, "that the God of our Lord Jesus Christ, the Father of glory, may give you a spirit of wisdom and of revelation in the knowledge of Him, having the eyes of your hearts enlightened" (vv. 17–18).

Since God is sovereign, we must pray to Him because salvation wholly depends on His gracious working and on the spiritual resources we cannot create, but that He alone is able to provide. Specifically, Paul realizes that we utterly depend on God giving His Holy Spirit to enliven and illuminate our hearts, to make us spiritually receptive, and to open blind eyes to the light that is shining. 1 Corinthians 2:14: "The natural person does not accept the things of the Spirit of God, for they are folly to him, and he is not able to understand them because they are spiritually discerned." This is why Paul so often prays both for the conversion of unbelievers and for the spiritual growth of believers, because the work of God's Spirit is necessary for both. Likewise, we must pray to the sovereign God for ourselves and for others, beseeching the Spirit's enlivening and illuminating work.

This raises a question: "Does prayer change God's will?" Is God's mind or attitude or purpose altered by our prayers? To understand prayer rightly, and its relationship to God's sovereignty, we must realize that the answer to this question is "No." Prayer does not change God's will.

There are people today who insist that if prayer does not change God's mind or will, then there is no need to pray and the Bible's emphasis on prayer is a sham. But far from being outraged at the idea that prayer does not change God's will, Christians should be profoundly grateful. God is, after all, all-wise. What wisdom might we contribute to His thinking that would produce a superior understanding? God is omniscient, that is, all-knowing. What information do we think that He lacks that we might provide to give Him more or better information? Likewise, God is completely holy. Do we really wish that we, being sinful and corrupt, could exert a moral influence on God's holiness? And what sort of influence do we think it might be? God's mind is informed by omniscience—perfect knowledge of all things, past, present, and future. Do we wish Him to change His mind based on our ignorance? For all these reasons, we should be glad that God is sovereign and that our prayers do not change His will.

Paul asks in Romans 11:34, "Who has known the mind of the Lord, or who has been His counselor?" The answer is "No one." Christian leaders glibly talk of our prayers shaping God's policy today; but if God's purpose is an eternal one, as Paul insists, then his policy is *not* being shaped today.[7] Our folly does not dictate to God's wisdom. Our sinfulness does not direct His holiness. Our ignorance does not overrule His perfect knowledge. If our prayers changed God's will, then we would be sovereign, not He, and His will could no longer be described as Paul does in Romans 12:2: "His good, pleasing and perfect will" (NIV).

Prayer does not change God's will. Now let me ask the question a different way: "Do our prayers change *things*?" Are there things that happen that would not have happened had we not prayed or if we had prayed for something different? Here the

---

[7] Cf. Arthur W. Pink, *The Sovereignty of God* (Grand Rapids: Baker, 1993), 168.

the answer is "Yes." Our prayers do change things, because God is sovereign and has ordained prayer as a means to the ends that He also has ordained. While prayer does not change God's will or plan, prayer is used by God within His will and plan. It is in this sense that he says to all His people, "Pray to Me, and I will hear you" (Jeremiah 29:12).

Even if prayer did not change circumstances it would still be worthwhile to pray, first, simply to praise God, but also because prayer changes us. Prayer changes our attitude to circumstances that God may not wish to change. Paul says, "In everything by prayer and supplication with thanksgiving let your requests be made known to God. And the peace of God, which surpasses all understanding, will guard your hearts and your minds in Christ Jesus" (Philippians 4:6-7). That alone is an important reason why we need to pray. People who insist that prayer only matters if God grants our wishes fail to appreciate the importance of worship and the value of the peace that God gives.

But prayer goes beyond changing us. It changes things, it changes events, it changes outcomes. Why? Because the God to whom we pray is sovereign—He is able to do all things—and He has ordained prayer as a means by which all He has ordained will come to pass. Therefore we should pray for our needs, for help, for relief, for God's power to overcome dangers and temptations, and to help us in our witness and ministry, because it is through our prayers that God intends to provide these things. As Martin Luther said, "Prayer is not overcoming God's reluctance, but laying hold of His willingness."[8]

---

[8] Cf. Arthur W. Pink, *The Sovereignty of God* (Grand Rapids: Baker, 1993), 169.

Sam Storms offers an example of how prayer serves as a means God has provided to accomplish salvation today. Suppose, he writes, God decided that a man named Gary will be saved through faith in Christ on August 8. Suppose also that, unbeknownst to me, God wills to bring him to faith in response to my prayer for Gary on August 7. Storms asks:

> Does this mean that God's will for Gary's salvation on the eighth might fail should I forget or refuse to pray on the seventh? No. We must remember that God has decreed or willed my praying on the seventh for Gary's salvation, which He intends to effect on the eighth. God does not will the end, that is, Gary's salvation on the eighth, apart from the means, that is, my prayer on the seventh. . . .From a human perspective, it may rightly be said that God's will for Gary is dependent upon me and my prayers, as long as it is understood that God, by an infallible decree, has secured and guaranteed my prayers as an instrument with no less certainty than He has secured and guaranteed Gary's faith as an end."[9] Why, some then will ask, should I bother praying, if it is all decreed by God? The answer, of course, is that I do not know what God has ordained until it happens. Having Gary's salvation on my heart, what else should I do but pray and use every other opportunity to lead him to faith and salvation, trusting that God will bless these means as He is so often glad to do?

Prayer does not change God, but it does change things, according to God's good and holy eternal counsel and sovereign will. Therefore, Paul sees an urgent need for prayer, and he prays that God will send the Holy Spirit to lead the Ephesians into a deeper knowledge of God.

---

[9] *Ibid.* 320.

**God's Sovereignty as an Encouragement to Prayer**

First, God's sovereignty gives us every *reason* to pray, as well as giving us every *need* to pray. Finally, we have every *encouragement* to pray, because Christ is exalted over all, exercising God's royal sovereignty for the church.

We will utterly fail to grasp Paul's emphasis in Ephesians 1 unless we realize that God's sovereignty is exercised in Christ and through Christ for our salvation. This means that if you want to know that God has chosen you for salvation, then you must come to Jesus Christ in faith. But it also means that if you belong to Christ, then God's sovereignty is exercised by Him who already has shown His unbounded love for you by dying on the cross for the forgiveness of your sins. This is why Paul ends the chapter by showing us Christ exalted: "He raised Him from the dead and seated Him at His right hand in the heavenly places, far above all rule and authority and power and dominion, and above every name that is named, not only in this age but also in the one to come" (1:20-21). God exalted Christ for a reason, namely to be sovereign "over all things [for] the church, which is His body, the fullness of Him who fills all in all" (vv. 22-23).

When we bow our heads and lift our hearts to God in the name of Jesus, that is the name of the sovereign One who sits at God's right hand in glory and power. The Son of God is enthroned as a man, knowing all too well what it is to sorrow and suffer, and to have need of God's help, grace, mercy, and power through the Holy Spirit.

Since God has exalted His Son, the man Jesus Christ, to the place of sovereignty, we are encouraged by His ability to understand our needs. Furthermore, since this is the same Lord Jesus who loved us and gave His life for our sins, we can be sure of His willingness to employ His divine power and authority for our sakes. Our prayers are received into hands that were pierced for us. What greater encouragement could we have about the welcome our prayers will receive in the courts of heaven? Paul reasons in Romans 5:10: "If while we were enemies we were reconciled to God by the death of His Son, how much more, now that we are reconciled, shall we be saved by His life?"

The story is told of a Civil War soldier who went to the White House with a pressing need with which he thought only the President could help him. To his dismay, he found a great number of people seeking an audience and a staff of assistants whose job was to keep them out. Dejected, the soldier fell into a seat, where a young boy came up to him and asked him why he felt so sad. The man replied, "I came a long way to see the President, but now I realize I won't be able to." The little boy grabbed him by the hand and led him past the guards and the staff of assistants, through a number of doors and into the oval office where the President was working. "Father," the boy said, "This soldier needs your help." Abraham Lincoln put down his pen, looked up, and said, "Certainly, my son. Now, my friend, what can I do to help you?" This is what it means to us that God's Son, Jesus Christ, is there in heaven, exalted for us, so that we will always have access in prayer to the heavenly Father.

### The Scepter Raised

If God is sovereign, why should we pray? We have every *reason* to pray because of the thanks we owe to God for His sovereign grace. We have every *need* to pray because of our whole reliance on the work of His Holy Spirit. But, above all this, we have every *encouragement* to pray because of our assurance of God's favor in Christ, His own Son and our Savior, who grants us unfailing access to the Father, and whom God has established as head over all for the sake of the church.

Every Wednesday night at the church where I serve, believers in Christ gather for a time of prayer together. The reason we do this is to worship and thank God for His blessings on our church and people, and then to pray for the work of God's kingdom and the needs of His people. What a need there is for a prayer meeting like this! What will happen to us, how will our needs be met, and what power will our ministry have, if we do not pray as a church? What an encouragement we have to gather for prayer because of the open access won for us by the saving work of God's Son, Jesus Christ.

There are believers who rise a bit earlier in the morning, or who set apart some other time of the day, to pray. They pray for family and friends. They pray for their children or their parents; husbands pray for wives and wives for their husbands. They pray for those in great need, those who are sick or out of work. They pray for the salvation of people they know, and they pray for opportunities to share the gospel clearly and with love. They pray for Christians suffering in faraway places. They pray for the church and the work of God's Word to convert sinners and lead people who are saved in paths of righteousness. Some of these people pray for me. You may be surprised to learn that people, many of them, have prayed for you as you read these words.

What about you? Do you labor in the courts of heaven with the power of prayer that has been given to you for the blessing of others and the service of God? Does it matter if you do? It most certainly matters, and it matters just as much when we do not pray. "You do not have," says James 4:2, "because you do not ask." "The prayer of faith will save the one who is sick," says James 5:15. And the prayer of one made righteous in Christ has great power (James 5:16).

There is a story in the Bible that speaks of the great privilege of access and favor that is ours in prayer. The story is that of

Esther, the beautiful Jewish girl who became Queen of Persia. The Book of Esther deals with a plot by the evil official Haman to have the Jews persecuted. Mordecai, Esther's uncle, incurred Haman's wrath and appealed for Esther to use her influence to protect God's people. Esther was afraid to act, because one could only approach the king in his inner court if first summoned by him. Anyone who approached the king without being summoned was required by law to be put to death (Esther 4:11). Only if the king, seeing him or her, extended his golden scepter, could the person be spared and admitted into his royal presence.

After three days of prayer and fasting, Esther summoned the resolve to go forward. First she put on her royal robes, and only then did she go into the king's inner chamber and stand before him. Esther 5:2-3 tells us what happened:

> When the king saw Queen Esther standing in the court, she won favor in his sight, and he held out to Esther the golden scepter that was in his hand. Then Esther approached and touched the tip of the scepter. And the king said to her, "What is it, Queen Esther? What is your request? It shall be given you, even to the half of my kingdom."

If that is the response of a pagan monarch towards his wife, how much more can we expect when we appear in Christ's name before the throne of our heavenly Father? Like Esther, we must be careful to come in the robe God has given us, the perfect righteousness of Jesus Christ, imputed to us through faith in His blood. Do you want to know how you can be right with God like that, so that your prayers are gladly accepted in heaven? You must trust in Jesus Christ, God's own Son, who died to pay the penalty your sins deserve and who through faith alone grants you His own robe of perfect righteousness. So, dressed as Christ's own bride, we shall surely be precious in His sight. And, with our Savior Jesus enthroned forever as Lord over all, we will find the scepter permanently raised for us. As Paul writes later in this epistle: "Through Him," that is, Christ, "we have access to the Father" (Ephesians 2:18).

Count Zinzendorff wrote: "Jesus, thy blood and righteousness, my beauty are, my glorious dress; midst flaming worlds, in these arrayed, with joy shall I lift up my head."[10] That will be true not only in the future, when in the Day of Judgment we ourselves come to stand before God's throne in the righteousness of Christ. It is also true now, as our prayers come to Jesus and are received into sovereign hands with love and care and joy. What a great *reason* we have to become a people of prayer! What great *need* there is for us to pray! And what an *encouragement* to come to God in the name of and through faith in the Lord Jesus Christ. To Him be glory forever.

---

[10] Nikolaus Ludwig von Zinzendorf, "Jesus, Thy Blood and Righteousness," 1739.

# "Christian" Prayer

## Hywel Jones

The term "Christian" is still used widely enough to be familiar, but it has lost much of its distinctive meaning. It is therefore
worth recalling that originally it referred to something quite
special. Luke, the sacred historian, provides an account of the
time and place of its first use, which was in Antioch in Syria
around 40-50 A.D. (see Acts 11:24).[1]

After the death of Stephen, Jews who believed in Jesus were
driven away from Jerusalem. Among those who went north and
then west around the corner of the Mediterranean Sea were
some who did not restrict the gospel message to Jews only. As a
result Greeks came to believe in Jesus of Nazareth as the Christ
(Messiah) of God and, together with believing Jews, they formed
a distinct social grouping in Antioch. It seems that they were
given the name "Christian" by others as a mark of opprobrium,
a mark of ignominy and reproach—at least that was how Herod
Agrippa II used it some twenty years later in response to Paul
about his preaching (see Acts 26:28), and how the Apostle Peter
used it when he spoke about suffering persecution (see 1 Peter
4:16). An interesting parallel to this name is found in the Gos-
pels where we read of some Jews who were termed "Herodians"
(see Matthew 22:16; Mark 3:6, 12:13) because of their support

---

[1] There was another name by which believers in Jesus as Lord were known.
"The Way", with its associations in the Old Testament and the teaching of
Jesus (Exodus 33:13; Psalm 119: Matthew 7:13-14; John 14:6) was probably
the church's preferred self-designation (see Acts 9:2; 19; 9, 23: 22:4; 24: 14,
22).

for Herod's dynasty. That being so, what could be more suitable than to describe those whose allegiance was primarily and openly to the "Christ" as "Christians." They were obviously not a Jewish sect. They may therefore be said to have invited the nickname, even though they did not coin it.

Luke's informative sidelight carries an important implication, namely that no one could have been called a Christian in the era before the coming of the promised Messiah (BC), but only in "the year of our Lord" (AD). All Old Testament believers were expecting God's messiah, but the best of them were uninformed about who he would be and when he would come (see 1 Peter 1:10–12). Everything "Christian" is therefore distinctive, and not only in relation to what is anti-Christian but also *in some way* from what is pre-Christian (see below). This progression in revelation is recognized whenever the relationship between the Testaments is under discussion. It is structured by the ideas of continuity and contrast. The subject of worship has received considerable attention over the last decades in this regard, but in that the matter of "prayer" has not been highlighted. A cursory glance at any prayer in the Old Testament, and any one found in Acts to Revelation in the New will show that there is indeed something to be investigated.[2] This is why the subject is being considered, and why the term is italicized in the heading of this essay.

In 2005 Bryan Chapell published a thought-provoking book on prayer with the striking title, "Praying *Backwards* in Jesus' Name"[3]. In doing so he had a twofold aim. Negatively, he

---

[2] As an example compare Genesis 18:22–33 or Ezra 8 or Psalm 84 with Ephesians 1:15–22.

[3] Bryan Chapell, *Praying Backwards in Jesus' Name: Transform Your Prayer Life by Beginning in Jesus' Name* ( Grand Rapids: Baker, 2005).

sought to discourage Christians from making use of the name of Jesus merely as a way of concluding a prayer that all too often amounted to little more than a list of individual (selfish?) interests and concerns. Positively, his conviction was that if people *began* their prayers by thinking about the name of Jesus, then their praying would be more in keeping with Christ's desires, and so with God's will. The sub-title of his book is *Transform Your Prayer Life by Beginning in Jesus' Name*—and from the several recommendations of the book it is clear that Chappell is not barking up a wrong tree. The same sort of conviction and concern animate this essay.

What, then, is distinctive about *Christian* praying? In the light of what has been said the answer to this question can only be found in the New Testament. It is supplied by our Lord in His address to His disciples on the eve of His Passion. In the Upper Room He twice described prayer as "asking the Father in [His] name" (see John 15:16 and 16:23) and told His disciples, "Until now you have asked nothing in My name" (16:24). This is a statement that should not be passed over, but noted and weighed. It is emphatic in its literary form; a double negative is used. Two things should be said about this intriguing clause, beginning with the obvious-but-perhaps perplexing truth that

**Asking the Father in [Christ's] name was something the disciples *had not* done.**

This is surprising when it is remembered that all the disciples were Jews and that they had "been with Jesus" (see Luke 3:14). As Jews, the Old Testament Scriptures in their entirety were theirs and they were familiar with daily prayers and synagogue worship on the Sabbath. In addition, some of them had been disciples of John the Baptist and had been taught a prayer by him (Luke 11:1). As disciples of Jesus they had observed and been impressed by His praying and had asked Him to teach them. He told them not to pray as the heathen and hypocrites did, but to address God as Father, being concerned about His glory and confident about His supply of all their needs, physical and spiritual (see Matthew 6:5-13; Luke 11:2-4). Jesus had also elucidated this prayer in the several parables that He told (see Luke 11:5-13; 18:1-14). But all this had not resulted in their asking the Father in His name. Early in the last century the Anglican New Testament scholar H. B. Swete drew attention to this by the remark that "The simpler precept and promise, 'Ask, and ye shall receive' belongs to the early teaching of the Ministry, but the condition 'in My name' was reserved to the end."[4]

We will concentrate our attention on John 16:18-26, where the idea of "asking" is prominent. Three different verbs, each of which could be translated by the one simple English word "ask", are used in the Greek text. The English Standard Version renders them uniformly by that term. It is however possible, given the context, that some variation in meaning could be present and that "asking questions" would be more suitable in some places and not "making requests". The New American Standard Bible uses the former in verses 19, 23, and 30, where the many questions that they had asked are recalled; and it is worth noting that ESV also has "question" in its rendering of verse 30. There is therefore some room for variation in the choice of English terms wherever it is suitable to the immediate context. "Asking the Father in Christ's name" is therefore quite different from asking Jesus questions as they had been doing, and even

---

[4] H.B. Swete, *The Last Discourse and Prayer of Our Lord* (London: MacMillan & Co., 1914) 141.

from asking God the LORD as in Old Testament prayers. But second, and to be fair to them,

> Asking the Father in [Christ's] name was something that they *could not* have done.

In all that Jesus said in the Upper Room His concern was to assure the disciples that His departure would be to their benefit and not to their loss. This applies to the words "until now you have asked for nothing in My name." They were not intended as a censure, but as a summary of the then state of affairs. This is seen by the fact that they were immediately followed by an assurance that the situation would soon be transformed. The disciples would be "asking the Father in His name," and, what is more, they would be answered abundantly! But their condition, disclosed by the questions they had asked, precluded their doing so at that time. This was not only due to their limited knowledge, but also and more importantly to the time in which they lived, which was pointed out to them in two main ways.

First, Jesus called them "little children" (13:33), and, while the diminutive form of the noun carries the note of affection, it also indicates a state of spiritual immaturity.[5] Their state of mind and heart was manifested by their inward agitation on account of His impending departure (14:1, 27); their impulsive protestations of loyalty (13:36-38) and knowledge (16:29-30) coupled with questions that display ignorance (13:7, 36-38; 14:5; 14:8; 14:22 and 16:17-18). They had immense difficulty in believing that His departure from them would be to their ad-

---

[5] The Apostle Paul uses the same analogy in Galatians 4:1-7 (v. 6 is linked with prayer).

vantage due to their preoccupation with the physical, the visible and the earthly (see 16:7)—thinking that was BC in character.

Second, Jesus used the expression "until now" indicating that something new was about to happen. Herman Ridderbos says that this expression "marks the change of dispensations"[6] The disciples were therefore living at that unique time in redemptive history when the old covenant was about to give way to the new. From the divine standpoint this transition would be natural, like a butterfly emerging from a chrysalis; from the human side it would be cataclysmic and traumatic (see Hebrews 12:27).[7] The disciples were about to pass through a religio-social and personal upheaval that was greater than both the Flood and the Babylonian Exile put together (see Isaiah 54:7-10). It is little wonder that they felt as if they were about to be orphaned (see 14:18). To mitigate their forsakenness Jesus amplified what He meant by "until now" by speaking to them about "a little while" and of "that day/hour."

### "A little while" verses 16–19

Jesus had used this expression as He began His pastoral address to His disciples about His imminent departure (see 13:33). Reminding them that He had spoken to the Jews of His removal and their fruitless search for Him (see 7:32-36; 12:35), He now says much the same to the disciples. But two differences should be noted. To His disciples Jesus does not say once, "you will not find Me," but He says twice, "a little while," and almost in the same breath. He does not say, "you will not find Me," because

---

[6] H.Ridderbos, *The Gospel of John: A Theological Commentary*. Trsl. J. Vriend (Grand Rapids: Wm. B. Eerdmans. 1991.

[7] See the summary of the changes that would result by J.I. Packer in *Fundamentalism and The Word of God* (London: IVF, 1958), 52-53.

He will look for them and find them when He "returns." He was therefore explaining to His mystified (but not unbelieving) disciples that He would not only leave, but return, and also how they would feel on both counts (16:16, 17, 19 and 25).

"A little while" therefore points to redemptive-historical events and corresponding personal experiences for the disciples. Jesus would be no longer visible to them and they would be sad; but then He would reappear and they would be glad. And that process would never be repeated! The joy that would banish their sadness would last forever (see vv. 20 and 22).

### "In that day" verses 23, 26

This is almost a technical expression in the Old Testament prophets along with "in those days" or "the latter days" or just "afterwards" as a preface for their predictions about the "Day of the Lord," the coming of the Messiah. Patterned after the Exodus from Egypt it would be His personal intervention at the end of time by which He would judge His foes and save His people. This coming is divided into two comings in the New Testament, *first* to save and *then* to judge. "In that day" therefore relates to both and embraces the interval between them that are the Last Days. They also stretch out into eternity. "That day" is therefore a description of an era, of *Anno Domini*. It has begun; it is ongoing and it will be consummated. Christians look back to it, live in it, and look forward to it because Jesus, the promised Messiah, is on the throne.

Jesus also used the noun "the hour" to describe it (16:25). He "constantly refers to His death on the cross and the exaltation [as] bound up with it (7:30, 8:20; 12:23, 27; 13:1 and 17:1), or the consequences deriving from it (5:28–29)".[8] The last hour

---

[8] D.A.Carson. *The Gospel According to John*. Nottingham: IVP. 171

on God's clock has therefore struck; the "end" has begun and there will never be another time-change. The day has dawned. "The darkness is passing away and the true light is shining" (see 1 John 2:8).

The fact that there is something redemptive-covenantal about this hour is underlined by Jesus' analogy of a woman about to give birth. This is not merely another picture of grief being turned to joy because it is one of the Old Testament metaphors connected with "the day of the Lord." Sadness being turned to gladness for the people of God (and even death being overcome by life) is associated with "that day" (see Isaiah 26:17, 18). Both Jesus and His disciples would experience those birth pangs that would bring in the new era, He of course more than they. He would be arrested and condemned; they would forsake Him and flee (v. 32). But He would conquer the world and bring them peace (v. 33).

With this laid down as a foundation we are now able to consider the positive statement that Jesus made to His disciples, which is that:

### Asking the Father in Christ's name was something that they *would* do.

While Jesus guaranteed this to His disciples with the words "you will ask in My name," He made it clear to them that they would only do so on "that day" when He would no longer speak to them in parables but "tell them plainly about the Father" (v. 26). "That day" was therefore not only bound up with the accomplishment of redemption by the Son, but it would also bring in an era of greater revelation by the Spirit. This is what is pointed to by the several uses of the comparative adjective "greater things" in the Gospel[9] and the somewhat cryptic statement that "the Spirit was not yet [given] because Jesus was not yet glorified" (John 7:38). At Pentecost a greater light began to shine for the disciples on Jesus' past teaching (see 14:26) and what He had not been able to teach them before (see 16:13-15). The Holy Spirit's ministry of bearing witness to the gospel keeps pace with the progress of redemptive revelation.

All the crucial events in the history of redemption are therefore encompassed in the expression "that day," together with their effects. This clearer and fuller revelation of God as Father that would be given to the disciples would lead them to think of Israel's God as revealed in His Son, Jesus, and to pray to Him in that light. The Holy Spirit would enlarge their understanding and deepen their joy and peace. Consequently, they would have more to pray about to the Father and to proclaim to the world. Instead of asking Jesus questions, they would make requests to the Father in His name—and call God "Father" in doing so.

A twofold proof of this progression is provided in the Acts of the Apostles. Immediately before His ascension the disciples ask Jesus the question, "Will you at this time restore the kingdom to Israel?" (see 1:6). This shows that their thinking was still BC in character, though they were now living in AD, so to speak. But after the outpouring of the Spirit on the Day of Pentecost such questions as "Where is Jesus? Why isn't He with us? Wouldn't it be better if He were? Where has He gone? Where is heaven? Why has He gone there? What is He doing there? Why doesn't He reveal God visibly, politically, territorially?" were not asked any more. (Would that the like were never heard in our churches!)

---

[9] See 1:50; 5:20 and 14:12.

What is unique about *Christian* prayer therefore is that it is the consequence of an accomplished redemption *and* a final revelation. An attempt must now be made to describe its features. This will be done by way of comment on the two other kinds of prayer that were highlighted by the adjectives "non-Christian" and "pre-Christian" at the beginning of this essay.

### Non-Christian Prayer

Prayer is a feature of all world religions and those of a home-spun variety. This is because though all human beings are fallen because of sin, they are made in the image of God, which cannot be totally eradicated. This *sensus divinitatis* survives even in atheists and agnostics.[10] Man is a dependent, sinful creature and thanksgivings for help, petitions for aid, and sacrifices to placate the gods are the proof of it. See the celebration of the Philistines (see Judges 16:23-24), the feverish flagellations of the prophets of Baal (see 1 Kings 18:25-26), the sailors on Jonah's ship (Jonah 1:5), and the desperate immolation of children (2 Kings 16:3 and Micah 6:7b). What Jesus said about the "many words" of the heathen is to the point here (see Matthew 6:7).[11]

Recognizing and referring to such activities as "prayer" is therefore a perfectly proper thing for Christians to do because it only means acknowledging a fact of life. Refusing to do so will seriously and unnecessarily hamper the church's witness in a multi-religious and pluralistic society. Doing so does not carry the implication that all praying is the same, nor justify participa-

---

[10] See B.B.Warfield's essay "God and Human Religion and Morals" in *Selected Shorter Writings Vol 1.* ed. John E. Meeter (Nutley, NJ: Presbyterian & Reformed Publishing Co., 1970), 41-45.

[11] See the most informative symposium *Teach Us To Pray: Prayer in the Bible and the World*, ed. D. A.Carson (World Evangelical Fellowship. Paternoster Press, 1990) .

tion in multi-religious services where the name of Jesus is excluded from public prayer. It must always be remembered that
"non-Christian prayer" *may* be the result of the stirring of the
sovereign Spirit as He draws sinners to the gospel of Jesus Christ
(see Job 33:14-30). Cornelius had to begin somehow and
somewhere before being led into more and more light (Acts 10-
11). Whatever may and should be said about his spiritual state
before Peter visited him, it is important to acknowledge that his
"prayers and alms [had] come up as a memorial before God"
(Acts 10:4), and yet "he needed to hear a message by which [he
could] be saved" (Acts 11:14).[12]

### Pre-Christian Prayer

There is a world of difference between this and non-
Christian prayer. Pre-Christian prayer is made in believing response to the Word of God as it was progressively revealed and
recorded in the course of Israel's history. Such prayers are addressed to the one true and living God who is the God of all the
earth, and also the LORD, the covenant Redeemer of His people. As is made clear, particularly in the Psalms, they extol His
glory, rehearse His saving deeds and sanctifying words in the
course of offering thanksgiving, seeking pardon, requesting aid,
and expressing consecration. They are offered to Him by faith in
His promises and in dependence on His grace and were favorably heard and answered.

So much in them, as in the rest of the Old Testament, trans-
fers itself with perfect ease into the New Testament because in
them the same God speaks about His one gospel (see Hebrews
1:1-3). Occasionally, however, some adjustment of focus must

---

[12] See the author's *Only One Way: Do People have to believe in Christ to be saved?*
(Leominster: Day One Publishing, 1996).

be made. The single greatest "correction" that is called for is in connection with those Psalms in which God's judgment of His and His people's foes is earnestly sought.[13] To treat these properly a pair of New Covenant spectacles (or lenses) is needed. These petitions are not vindictive outbursts, but an awareness of the malignity of all opposition to God and a longing for Him to be honored. They have their parallels elsewhere in the Old Testament, and also in the New (see Revelation 6:10; 11:17-18, and 19:1-2).

Such prayers, however, relate to judgment at the end of all things (that will take place at the Second Coming of Christ) and not to His incarnation, the purpose of which sharpens or clarifies the Old Testament prediction and expectation. Instead of a single intervention of God to judge and save, the Messiah came not to condemn, but to save the world (John 3:15-16). But He will come again to judge the ungodly and the impenitent. Such a distinction could not be made BC, but only AD. The godly in Israel could not make this adjustment even during the earthly ministry of Jesus. John the Baptist, who announced His coming as the world's sin-bearer, failed to understand this because he belonged to the era of "the law and the prophets" (see Matthew 11:2-15, especially vv. 11-15). Jesus' disciples were also not clear on this (see Luke 9:54).

### The Lord's Prayer: Pre-Christian or Christian?

At this point a word about how what is known as "The Lord's Prayer" should be regarded and used is appropriate. Rightfully, it has been given an important place in Christian

---

[13] See, for example, Psalm 139:19-21 and Nehemiah 4:4-5. The historical accounts of the slaughter of pagan nations that has been so objected to is to be regarded in the same way.

thinking and over the years in her worship of God. Disagree-
ment was strong in the 17<sup>th</sup> century over whether its use was es-
sential in worship, especially when the secular powers made it
obligatory in the Act of Uniformity of 1662. John Owen, the
English Puritan, wrote a treatise entitled "A Discourse Concerning Liturgies and their Imposition." In it he said:

> Our Saviour did command that form to be repeated by his
> disciples" . . . [but] at that time [he] was minister of the
> Circumcision, and taught the doctrine of the gospel under
> and with the observation of all the worship of the Judaical
> church. He was not yet glorified and so the Spirit was not
> as yet given . . .which he promised unto his disciples to en-
> able them to perform all the worship of God by him re-
> quired at their hands . . . [so the old form] seems to have
> belonged unto the economy of the Old Testament.[14]

R. L. Dabney, the 19<sup>th</sup> century Southern Presbyterian theologian, set aside its use in public worship, but regarded it as "a
general guide in the structure of our own petitions and as a
form whose very words are to be employed by us on proper occasions." He supported his position as follows:

> [The] most plausible objection to it, as a model for Chris-
> tians is that it contains no express reference to a Mediator,
> and answer through His merit and intercession. The an-
> swer is that it is an Old Testament prayer: is intended as
> such because that dispensation was still standing. When it
> was about to close, Christ completed this feature of it, by

---

[14] John Owen, "A Discourse Concerning Liturgies and their Imposition,"
*Works*, vol. 15 chapter 3

enjoining the use of His name. See John 14:13; 15:16; 16:23-24.[15]

Samuel Miller, colleague of Archibald Alexander in Princeton, argues likewise and says:

> To adopt it now as containing all that is necessary to constitute a complete prayer under the full light and claims and privileges of the New Testament economy must surely be considered as a virtual desertion of principles which, as Christians, under the present dispensation we must ever acknowledge and hold fast viz. that the kingdom of heaven, or the gospel dispensation is already come; and that no Christian prayer is complete which does not include a reference to the merits and intercession of the great High Priest of our profession.[16]

It therefore seems that the principle that we are using in this essay about the distinction between the old and new dispensations of the covenant of grace in relation to prayer has been recognized. Discussion about the propriety of the use of the Lord's Prayer in public worship will doubtless continue, but there can be no doubt that it should be used by Christians as a guide to all their praying.[17] Calvin's comment on it is well worth remembering as well as recording. He wrote:

> This prayer is in all respects so perfect that any extraneous or alien thing added to it, which cannot be related to it, is

---

[15] R. L. Dabney, *Systematic Theology* (Edinburgh: Banner of Truth Trust, 1985), 721.

[16] *Thoughts on Public Prayer* pp.51-54

[17] See *A Method for Prayer* by Matthew Henry and also the expositions of it in the Heidelberg and Westminster Catechisms. Also the expositions of the Lord's Prayer by Thomas Watson and Herman Witsius.

> impious and unworthy to be approved by God. For in this
> summary he has set forth what is worthy of him, acceptable
> to him, necessary for us—in effect, what he would willingly
> grant.[18]

It should, however, not be forgotten that he did not restrict
true and acceptable prayer only to the use of its words as a form.
He acknowledged that there were many others in the Bible
whose words were "far different from it . . . yet composed by the
same Spirit, the use of which is very profitable to us" and, what
is more, he adds: "Many prayers are suggested to believers by the
same Spirit, which bear little similarity [to it] in wording." The
all-important factor is that the "sense does not vary" though "the
words are utterly different."[19] The Lord's Prayer can be regarded
as a distillation of all such prayers in the Old Testament and the
mold for New Testament prayers—and "Christian" prayer until
Christ returns.

### "Christian" Prayer

This is "praying to God as Father in the name of Jesus." In
the Old Testament "Name" not only represents the one who
bears it, but also, especially if it is one subsequently given, to a
role in the purpose of God, for example Abraham and Sarah.[20]
"Name" is equivalent to the LORD God being present and ac-
tive to save. Jesus is the sent one of the Father, His Christ, because He came in [His] Father's name and not His own (see
John 5:43). So to pray to the Father in His name is to own Him

---

[18] *Institutes* Book III Chap 20. 48, Battles Translation.

[19] Ibid., 49.

[20] See the Article on "Name" By J. Alec Motyer in the *New Bible Dictionary*,
ed. J. D. Douglas, (London: IVF, 1962).

as Prophet, Priest and King, and to serve Him by way of adoration, confession, thanksgiving, and supplication.

In his inspiring (as well as instructive) chapter on "Prayer which is the chief exercise of faith, and by which we daily receive God's benefits," Calvin connects prayer with faith in Jesus Christ the Mediator, and also with the aid of the Holy Spirit as promised in the gospel. The believer is therefore told in God's Word that:

> Whatever we need and whatever we lack is in God, and in our Lord Jesus Christ in whom the Father willed all the fullness of his bounty to abide (Col.1:19; John 1:16) so that we may all *draw from it as from an overflowing spring*. . . [and] just as faith is born from the gospel, so through it our hearts are trained to call upon God's name (Romans 10:14-17). And . . . the Spirit of adoption, who seals the witness of the gospel in our hearts (Romans 8:16) *raises up our spirits* to dare to show forth to God their desires, to stir up unspeakable groaning (Romans 8:26) and confidently cry, "Abba! Father! (Romans 8:15) [21]

So Christian prayer is "draw[ing] from [Christ] an overflowing spring" and having one's "spirit raised" by the Holy Spirit as one comes to God as one's heavenly Father. This language belongs to the new covenant era, and Calvin is concerned to do this justice in dealing with John 16:24, 26 while maintaining that the prayers of Old Testament saints were heard and an-

---

[21] *Institutes*,III.20.18.

swered favorably as a retrospective benefit of "the Mediator's grace."[22] Commenting on John 16:26 he writes:

> And we ought carefully to note the circumstance of the time when Christ enjoins his disciples to take refuge in his intercession [namely that it is] after he shall have ascended into heaven. "In that hour", he says, "you will ask in my name."

He then faces John 16:24 and writes:

> Why then does Christ assign a new hour wherein His disciples shall begin to pray in His name unless it is that His grace, as it is more resplendent today, so deserves more approval among us . . . . [the disciples] did not yet clearly understand that Christ by His ascension into heaven would be *a surer advocate* of the church than He had been before." *(emphasis mine)* [23]

So knowing that one has a "surer advocate" and having one's "spirit raised" as one comes to God is what marks out "Christian" prayer. They are the consequence of the distinct but complementary ministries of two advocates, one before the throne of God in heaven for the believer guaranteeing access to God as Father (see 1 John 2:1, 2), and the other in the believer assuring him that he is a child and heir of God (Romans 8:15–28). The mediation of the Son and the ministry of the Spirit were under a veil in the Old Testament, but they are the hall-

---

[22] He explains this as being grounded on "that foreshadowing ceremony of the law [which] taught [them] that [they were] all barred from God's presence and consequently need a Mediator . . . Hence we infer that God was from the beginning appeased by Christ's intercession, so that he received the petitions of the godly."

[23] Ibid III 20.18

mark of the new covenant.[24] The result is that the believer is given boldness as he tells his heavenly Father everything with words and sighs.[25]

The words come from the whole of Scripture, Old and New, as the Spirit of Truth, their ultimate Author, brings its promises and precepts to mind and conscience, inspiring and directing meditation on them.[26] The Bible is to come alive as one prays as well as when one reads it in private and in public. There are times when such thoughts "will lie too deep" for words, and will only find vent in sighs and even tears occasioned by the "sufferings of this present time" as they affect the believer, the church, and the world. This non-verbal language is understood by the Spirit and translated by Him to the Father through the Son. Calvin says that He "arouses in us assurance, desires and sighs, to conceive which our natural powers would scarcely suffice."[27] This is what is meant by "praying in the Spirit" (Ephesians 6:18).

Three areas of this "praying in the Spirit" must be mentioned in closing. They are that it is trinitarian in shape, universal in scope, and childlike in spirit. The Old Testament is not silent on any of these, but they can only be seen to advantage in the New Testament Scriptures from Acts to Revelation. They are incipiently present in the prayer of the church at Jerusalem

---

[24] The Apostle Paul makes this clear in 2 Corinthians 3.

[25] See John Owen's masterly treatise on "The Work of the Holy Spirit in Prayer" in *The Works of John Owen*, vol. 4 (Edinburgh: Banner of Truth Trust, 1967).. (This has been abridged in a Puritan paperback by R. J. K. Law and published by the Trust in 1998.

[26] Here lies something of the value of regular Bible reading according to a plan and the memorization of texts and also of walking with God on one's pilgrimage through this wilderness of a world.

[27] *Institutes* III. 20. 5

recorded in Acts 4:22–30, which shows that Christian prayer looks just like Old Testament prayer, filtered and filled out by new covenant realities and language.

### Trinitarian in shape

What is meant by this is that in the doxologies, benedictions, wishes, and recorded prayers of the New Testament links are made between the Divine Persons that create a mold for later creedal formulation. In them primacy is given to the Father, with the Son being referred to (alongside Him sometimes) and with some mention of the Spirit's work. This is standard in the writings of the apostles Peter, John, and especially Paul. The latter generally addresses the Father and the Son, and does so by the Spirit, even laying down the declaration "through Him [Jesus Christ] we both [Jew and Gentile] have access in one Spirit to the Father" (Ephesians 2:18), and announces the benediction "the grace of the Lord Jesus Christ, the love of God, and the fellowship of the Holy Spirit" (2 Corinthians 16:14). Although this is an explication of the Divine Name "LORD" (the one who hears in heaven, comes down to save His people, and leads out of bondage and into a land flowing with milk and honey), it had to await the "hour and the day" before it could be made explicit.

### Universal in scope

It goes without saying that Christians pray for churches and fellow believers. The prayers that are recorded in the New Testament Epistles, and those that are asked for in them, are proof of this. Even John's words, "I do not say that one should pray for that" (see 1 John 5:16), occur in the context of encouraging prayer for fellow Christians who sin. But the world is also to be included in such intercession. The Old Testament does not confine God's goodness and grace to Israel alone. "The LORD is good to all and His mercy is over all that He has made" (Psalm 145:9). All people should pray to Him, but even when they do not "He is kind to the unthankful and the evil" (Luke 6:35). Job and Rahab, the widow of Zarephath, and the Ninevites are all examples of this. But in *Anno Domini* this is even plainer. God loves His enemies, in that He is kind to them (Matthew 5:44-45). He sent His son to die for a bad world of perishing human beings (John 3:16). His benevolent concern and activity is not limited to the church. Paul therefore urges that all sorts of prayers are to be prayed for all sorts of people in keeping with his desire that the gospel should be made known to all the nations. The gospel is to be freely preached to all, far and wide, and a ministry of "neighborly" intercession supports such proclamation. "This is good and it is pleasing in the sight of God our Savior [benefactor], who desires all people to be saved and to come to a knowledge of the truth" (see 1 Timothy 2:1-7).

### Childlike in spirit

If there is one feature of Christian prayer that distinguishes it from all else it is that in it God is addressed as "Father." Old Testament believers were humble and trusting, but God was only "father" to the king and to the nation (Exodus 4:22 and Isaiah 63:16). By contrast Jesus gives each believer the right to call His Father theirs (Luke 11:2 and John 20:17), and also gives His Spirit to enable them to do so (Romans 8:15 and Galatians 4:6).

And also we have the sure promise that God will hear and answer their prayers—always! He can no more turn a deaf ear to His children than He can to their Elder Brother who is at His right hand in heaven. The Father sent His Son to gather His estranged children and bring them home. He therefore delights to hear them call on His name in faith and love (whatever words they use, and in whatever language), and to respond positively to them.

They pray according to His Word; He replies according to His will. These two are not diverse because He has expressed His will in His Word so that his children may know what pleases Him. They can therefore, in so many cases, be sure that they are asking the Father for what He wants to give them, and that He will do so. They know that He has made abundant provision for all their needs and that He knows best what to give and when. They can therefore trust because they know they will never be orphaned—and one day they will be amazed at how their unworthy prayers have been answered.

And so, having taught His disciples *what* to say in prayer (Luke 11:2-4), Jesus went on to tell them *how* to say it. By means of two mini-parables He assured them that His Father and theirs will be better than a man's best friend, and much better than the best human father. He will never mind being disturbed, nor will His answers mock their prayers (see Luke 11:5-12). He will give the Holy Spirit and the good gifts of the kingdom of grace and glory to them (see Luke 11:13).

# The Concert of Prayer in the 18<sup>th</sup> Century:
## A Model for Praying Together
### Michael A. G. Haykin

Central to any expression of biblical spirituality is prayer. It is not surprising, therefore, that the Puritans, men and women who sought to frame their lives according to God's Word, wrote a great deal about this subject and were themselves, in the words of John Geree (c.1601-1649), "much in prayer."[1] As the Congregationalist theologian Thomas Goodwin (1600-1680) remarked, "our speaking to God by prayers, and His speaking to us by answers thereunto, is one great part of our walking with God."[2] John Bunyan (1628-1688) made a similar judgment about prayer's vital importance when he told those gathered to hear his final words as he lay dying in London, "The Spirit of Prayer is more precious than treasure of gold and silver."[3]

---

[1] John Geree, *The Character of an old English Puritan or Non-Conformist* (London, 1646) in Lawrence A. Sasek, *Images of English Puritanism. A Collection of Contemporary Sources 1589-1646* (Baton Rouge, LA/Louisiana State University Press, 1989), 209. It is also available at www.cet.com/~mtr/GereeChar.html.

[2] "The Return of Prayers," *The Works of Thomas Goodwin, D.D.* (Edinburgh: James Nichol, 1862), III, 362.

[3] "Mr. John Bunyan's Dying Sayings," *The Works of John Bunyan*, vol. I (Philadelphia: John Ball, 1850), 47.

## Jonathan Edwards: A Man of Prayer

Jonathan Edwards (1703-1758), America's greatest theologian, one who was very much a part of this stream of Puritan
and Reformed piety, also highly prized prayer. There can be
found, for example, among his *Resolutions*, this one dated July 23
and August 10, 1723 that declares his awareness of the believer's
life-long duty to pray:

> Resolved, very much to exercise myself in this, all my life
> long, viz. with the greatest openness, of which I am capable
> of, to declare my ways to God, and lay open my soul to
> him: all my sins, temptations, difficulties, sorrows, fears,
> hopes, desires, and every thing, and every circumstance;
> according to Dr. Manton's 27th Sermon on Psalm 119.[4]

The statement to which he is referring from the Puritan
author Thomas Manton (1620-1677) can be found in the doctrinal assertion of his twenty-seventh sermon on Psalm 119, in
which he states: "They that would speed with God, should learn
this point of Christian ingenuity, unfeignedly to lay open their
whole case to him."[5]

Early on in his ministry Edwards addressed in his sermon
*The Most High A Prayer-Hearing God* (1736) the subject of why
God had instituted prayer. First, Edwards takes note that of the
fact that the institution of prayer is not because God is ignorant
of our wants or desires. "He is omniscient," Edwards reminds
his hearers of a basic theological point, "and with respect to His

---

[4] *Jonathan Edwards' Resolutions And Advice to Young Converts*, ed. Stephen J.
Nichols (Phillipsburg, New Jersey: P&R Publishing, 2001), 26.

[5] "Letters and Personal Writings," ed. George S. Claghorn (*The Works of
Jonathan Edwards*, vol. 16; New Haven/ London: Yale University Press, 1998),
758, n.5.

knowledge, unchangeable."[6] Nor do we pray in order to alter God's sovereign will. Edwards is well aware of the anthropomorphic language of Scripture and admits: "God is sometimes represented as if He were moved and persuaded by the prayers of His people; yet it is not to be thought that God is properly moved or made willing by our prayers; for it is no more possible that there should be any new inclination or will in God than new knowledge."[7] Why, then, are Christians commanded to pray? Well, working from the Reformation principle that God alone can do the work of God,[8] Edwards states that "God has been pleased to constitute prayer to be antecedent to the bestowment of mercy, and He is pleased to bestow mercy in consequence of prayer, as though He were prevailed upon by prayer." As Stephen J. Nichols writes with regard to this passage:

> In other words, God ordains the end or the results, and he also ordains the means. Prayer is a God-ordained means to carrying out his will. Although this humbles us, God ordains the means of the prayers of his people in the carrying out of his will. We don't pray to change his mind; we pray so that we can be used of him.[9]

Sincere prayer also furthers the glorification of God, the goal of all creation. As Edwards puts it, "prayer is but a sensible acknowledgment of our dependence on Him to His glory."

---

[6] "The Most High A Prayer-Hearing God", *The Works of Jonathan Edwards* (1834 ed.; repr. Edinburgh: The Banner of Truth Trust, 1974), 2:115.

[7] Ibid., 115-116.

[8] Robert O. Bakke, *The Power of Extraordinary Prayer* (Wheaton, Illinois: Crossway Books, 2000), 123.

[9] *Jonathan Edwards: A Guided Tour of His Life and Thought* (Phillipsburg, New Jersey: P&R Publishing, 2001), 210.

Prayer is also designed to put those who pray in a proper frame of mind and heart to receive answers to their requests. Prayer changes those who pray, preparing them to be the sort of people through whom God can work.

> Fervent prayer many ways tends to prepare the heart. Hereby is excited a sense of our need, and of the value of the mercy which we seek, and at the same time earnest desires for it, whereby the mind is more prepared to prize it, to rejoice in it when bestowed, and to be thankful for it. Prayer, with suitable confession, may excite a sense of our unworthiness of the mercy we seek. And the placing of ourselves in the immediate presence of God, may make us sensible of his majesty, and in a sense fit to receive mercy of him. Our prayer to God may excite in us a suitable sense and consideration of our dependence on God for the mercy we ask, and a suitable exercise of faith in God's sufficiency, that so we may be prepared to glorify his name when the mercy is received.[10]

Finally, due to the fact that Edwards was persuaded that "the great duty of secret prayer. . .is more expressly required in the Word of God than any other kind" of prayer, he believed it was the duty of Christians to

> be much employed in the duty of prayer. Let us pray with all prayer and supplication. Let us live prayerful lives, continuing instant in prayer, watching thereunto with all perseverance. Praying always, without ceasing, earnestly, and not fainting.[11]

---

[10] "The Most High A Prayer-Hearing God," Works, 2:116.
[11] "The Most High A Prayer-Hearing God," Works, 2:116.

## The Concert of Prayer

One area of prayer that Edwards came to increasingly believe was vital for the expansion of God's kingdom was corporate prayer. While in some respects he was an innovator in his own time with regard to corporate prayer meetings, what he called "concerts of prayer," there was some Puritan precedent. For example, the New England Puritan Cotton Mather (1663-1728) believed that the vitality of the Church in any era is, in the final analysis, dependent on the Holy Spirit's sovereign power. He thus maintained that the most significant practical response to the spiritual decline of his day was concerted prayer. As he stated in *The Nets of Salvation* (1704):

> Praying for souls is a main stroke in the winning of souls. If once the Spirit of Grace be poured out upon a soul, that soul is won immediately. . . .Yea, who can tell, how far the prayers of the saints, & of a few saints, may prevail with heaven to obtain that grace, that shall win whole peoples and kingdoms to serve the Lord?. . . .It may be, the nations of the world, would quickly be won from the idolatries of paganism, and the impostures of Mahomet, if a Spirit of Prayer, were at work among the people of God.[12]

A later booklet from the pen of Mather, *Private Meetings Animated & Regulated*, which was published in 1706, encouraged believers to meet in small groups so that, among other things, "their fervent supplications" would hopefully result in "the Spirit of Grace [being] mightily poured out upon the rising generation." Mather recommended bi-monthly meetings in which the whole evening could be devoted "unto Supplications for the

---

[12] Cited Richard F. Lovelace, *The American Pietism of Cotton Mather: Origins of American Evangelicalism* (Grand Rapids: Wm. B. Eerdmans Publ. Co., 1979), 244.

Conversion and Salvation of the Rising Generation in the Land;
and particularly for the Success of the Gospel in that Congregation" to which the members of the prayer-meeting belonged.[13] It
is noteworthy that, though Mather prayed long and hard for
revival, he never personally saw it. He died in 1728, a few years
before it came to New England and Great Britain. Yet he typi-
fies a rising hunger among God's people in the transatlantic
British community to see God move in revival in their society,
and who translated that longing into prayer.

Jonathan Edwards' involvement in the Northampton revival
of 1734-1735 and the Great Awakening of 1740-1742 left him
with the keen conviction that the advance of God's kingdom in
history was intimately connected to such times of spiritual blessing. The New England divine was also certain that prayer for
these times of spiritual awakening was central to seeing them
take place. Thus, he drew up and published in 1748 a treatise
that sought to encourage believers to gather together regularly to
pray for the pouring out of God's Spirit. Entitled *An Humble
Attempt to Promote Explicit Agreement and Visible Union of God's
People in Extraordinary Prayer, For the Revival of Religion and the
Advancement of Christ's Kingdom on Earth, pursuant to Scripture-
Promises and Prophecies concerning the Last Time* (henceforth referred to simply as the *Humble Attempt*), the treatise is well
summed up by a sentence near the beginning of the work:

> It is a very suitable thing, and well-pleasing to God, for
> many people, in different parts of the world, by express
> agreement, to come into a visible union in extraordinary,
> speedy, fervent, and constant prayer, for those great effu-
> sions of the Holy Spirit, which shall bring on that ad-

---

[13] *Private Meetings Animated & Regulated* (Boston, 1706), 10-11, 19.

vancement of Christ's church and kingdom, that God has
so often promised shall be in the latter ages of the world.[14]

This treatise would have some impact during Edwards' own
lifetime, but its main influence came during the final decades of
the eighteenth century, when it was instrumental in kindling a
profoundly significant revival among the Calvinistic Baptists of
Great Britain and initiating the modern missionary movement.[15]

## The Humble Attempt

The *Humble Attempt* itself was inspired by information that
Edwards received during the course of 1745 about a prayer
movement for revival that had been formed by a number of
Scottish evangelical ministers, including such regular corre-
spondents of Edwards as John McLaurin (1693-1754) of the
Ramshorn Church, Glasgow, William McCulloch (1691-1771)
of Cambuslang, James Robe (1688-1753) of Kilsyth, and John
Erskine (1721-1803), then of Kirkintilloch. These ministers and
their congregations had agreed to spend a part of Saturday evening and Sunday morning each week, as well as the first Tues-
day of February, May, August, and November, in prayer to God
for "an abundant effusion of His Holy Spirit" so as to "revive
true religion in all parts of Christendom, and to deliver all nations from their great and manifold spiritual calamities and miseries, and bless them with the unspeakable benefits of the king-

---

[14] "Humble Attempt," *Apocalyptic Writings*, ed. Stephen J. Stein (*The Works
of Jonathan Edwards*, vol. 5 (New Haven/London: Yale University Press,
1977), 320.

[15] See Michael A. G. Haykin, *One heart and one soul: John Sutcliff of Olney,
his friends and his times* (Darlington, Co. Durham: Evangelical Press, 1994),
153-171.

dom of our glorious Redeemer, and fill the whole earth with his glory."[16] This "concert of prayer" ran for an initial two years, and then was renewed for a further seven.

When Edwards was sent information regarding it, he lost no time in seeking to implement a similar concert of prayer in the New England colonies. He encouraged his own congregation to get involved, and also communicated the concept of such a prayer union to neighboring ministers whom he felt would be receptive to the idea. Although the idea initially met with a poor response, Edwards was not to be put off. In a sermon given in February, 1747, on Zechariah 8:20-22, he sought to demonstrate how the text supported his call for a union of praying Christians. Within the year a revised and greatly expanded version of this sermon was ready for publication as the *Humble Attempt*.

The *Humble Attempt* is divided into three parts. The first section opens with a number of observations on Zechariah 8:20-22 and then goes on to provide a description of the origin of the concert of prayer in Scotland. From the text in Zechariah Edwards infers that "there shall be given much of a spirit of prayer to God's people, in many places, disposing them to come into an express agreement, unitedly to pray to God in an extraordinary manner, that He would appear for the help of His church, and in mercy to mankind, and pour out His Spirit, revive His work, and advance His spiritual kingdom in the world, as He has promised."[17] Edwards thus concludes that it is a duty well-pleasing to God, and incumbent upon God's people in America, to assemble and, with "extraordinary, speedy, fervent and

---

[16] "Humble Attempt," *Apocalyptic Writings*, ed. Stein, 321.

[17] Ibid., *Apocalyptic Writings*, ed. Stein, 317.

constant prayer," pray for those "great effusions of the Holy Spirit" that will dramatically advance the kingdom of Christ.

Part II of the treatise cites a number of reasons for participating in the concert of prayer. Our Lord Jesus shed His blood and tears, and poured out His prayers to secure the blessed presence of His Spirit for His people. "The sum of the blessings Christ sought," writes Edwards, "by what He did and suffered in the work of redemption, was the Holy Spirit." He then continues: "The Holy Spirit, in His indwelling, His influences and fruits, is the sum of all grace, holiness, comfort and joy, or, in one word, of all the spiritual good Christ purchased for men in this world; and is also the sum of all perfection, glory and eternal joy, that He purchased for them in another world."[18] Therefore, Edwards rightly concludes, if this is what Christ longed for and "set His heart upon, from all eternity, and which He did and suffered so much for, offering up 'strong crying and tears' [Hebrews 5:7], and His precious blood to obtain it; surely His disciples and members should also earnestly seek it, and be much and earnest in prayer for it."[19]

Scripture, moreover, is replete with commands, incentives, and illustrations regarding prayer for the Holy Spirit. There is, for example, the encouragement given in Luke 11:13.[20] These words of Christ, Edwards observes, imply that prayer for the Holy Spirit is one request that God the Father is particularly pleased to answer in the affirmative. Or one might consider the example of the early disciples who devoted themselves to "united fervent prayer and supplication. . .till the Spirit came

---

[18] Ibid., 341.

[19] Ibid., 344.

[20] "If ye then, being evil, know how to give good gifts unto your children, how much more shall your heavenly Father give the Holy Spirit to them that ask him?"

down in a wonderful manner upon them," as is related in Acts 1-2.[21]

Additional incentives to take part in the concert of prayer are provided by what Edwards terms "the spiritual calamities and miseries of the present time." Among them are the disastrous attempt by Charles Edward Stuart, Bonnie Prince Charlie, to seize the British throne for his father only a couple of years before in 1745-1746, the persecution of the Calvinistic Huguenots in France, the decay of vital piety, the deluge of vice and immorality, the loss of respect for those in vocational ministry, and the prevalence of religious fanaticism.[22] Edwards also sees in the drift of the intellectual and theological currents of his day a further reason for prayer, as men and women rejected Puritan theology so as to embrace theologies shaped by the rationalistic world-view of the Enlightenment:

> Never was an age wherein so many learned and elaborate treatises have been written in proof of the truth and divinity of the Christian religion; yet never were there so many infidels among those that were brought up under the light of the gospel. It is an age, as is supposed, of great light, freedom of thought, and discovery of truth in matters of religion, and detection of the weakness and bigotry of our ancestors, and of the folly and absurdity of the notions of those that were accounted eminent divines in former generations; which notions, it is imagined, did destroy the very foundations of virtue and religion, and enervate all precepts of morality, and in effect annul all difference between virtue and vice; and yet vice and wickedness did never so prevail, like an overflowing deluge. 'Tis an age wherein those mean and stingy principles (as they are called) of our forefathers, which (as is supposed) deformed

---

[21] Ibid., 347-348, 356.
[22] Ibid., 357-359.

religion, and led to unworthy thoughts of God, are very much discarded, and grown out of credit, and supposed more free, noble and generous thoughts of the nature of religion, and of the Christian scheme, are entertained; but yet never was an age, wherein religion in general was so much despised and trampled on, and Jesus Christ and God Almighty so blasphemed and treated with open daring contempt.[23]

Yet Edwards can list a number of events which show that, though his time is a "day of great apostasy," it is also a "day of the wonderful works of God; wonders of power and mercy" that should move believers to united prayer just as much as distresses and calamities.[24] Edwards especially highlights such "wonders of power and mercy" as the various spiritual revivals on the European continent—including one in Rotterdam in which a Scottish pastor, Hugh Kennedy (1698-1764) played a key role[25]—in Great Britain, and among the New England colonies. These "late remarkable religious awakenings," Edwards observes, "may justly encourage us in prayer for the promised glorious and universal outpouring of the Spirit of God."[26]

The beauty and benefits involved in a visible union for prayer is yet another motive Edwards gives for complying with his proposal. Unity, Edwards maintains, is regarded by the Scriptures as "the peculiar beauty of the church of Christ."[27] In support of this statement, Edwards refers his readers to Song of Songs 6:9, Psalm 122:3, and Ephesians 4:3-6, 16. Union in prayer would also prove to be beneficial for the church in that it

---

[23]Ibid., 359.
[24] Ibid., 362.
[25] Ibid., 289, n.3.
[26] Ibid., 363-364.
[27] Ibid., 364-365.

would tend to promote closer rapport between the members of different denominational bodies. In Edwards' words: "Union in religious duties, especially in the duty of prayer, in praying one with and for another, and jointly for their common welfare, above almost all other things, tends to promote mutual affection and endearment."[28]

Part III is the longest portion of the *Humble Attempt* and is devoted to answering various objections to the idea of a concert of prayer. Much of this section of the *Humble Attempt* is devoted to proving his case from a post-millennial reading of New Testament eschatology.[29] But it was also charged that the concert of prayer was something previously unknown in the history of the Church. It was thus suspect. In actual fact, there had been advocates for such meetings from the early years of the eighteenth century, for instance, Cotton Mather, as we have seen. Edwards makes no mention of Mather, but he does recall that in 1712 a group of London Dissenters had issued *A Serious Call from the City to the Country*, in which it was urged that an extra hour be set aside every week to beseech God to "appear for the Deliverance and Enlargement of His Church."[30]

A significant number of congregations in America and Scotland observed concerts of prayer throughout the 1750s. Especially during the French and Indian War (1755-1760), when the British and the French were fighting for the hegemony of North America, the concert of prayer was in wide use among American

---

[28]Ibid., 366.

[29] For a concise summary of Edwards' eschatology with regard to his advocacy of the concert of prayer, see Bakke, *Power of Extraordinary Prayer*, 56-62.

[30] "Humble Attempt," 428); Michael J. Crawford, *Seasons of Grace. Colonial New England's Revival Tradition in Its British Context* (New York: Oxford University Press, 1991), 41-42. See also Crawford, *Seasons of Grace*, 229, for further examples.

Calvinists. In 1759, for instance, Robert Smith informed fellow Presbyterians in Pennsylvania that the concert of prayer would prove to be far more effective in hastening the "brightest period of the militant Church's glory" than the military victories won by British forces.[31] Yet, as has been noted, the *Humble Attempt* would bear its greatest fruit some twenty-five years after the death of its author.

In essence, the *Humble Attempt* is a call for a practical expression of Reformation theology, which maintains that only God is able to do the work of God.[32] Believing this, the church has only one posture: prayer.

### The Prayer Call of 1784

In the spring of 1784, an English Baptist pastor John Ryland, Jr. (1753-1825) shared with his two closest friends and fellow pastors, John Sutcliff (1752-1814) and Andrew Fuller (1754-1815), this treatise of Edwards that we have been considering. It had been sent to him by the Scottish Presbyterian minister John Erskine (1721-1803). When Erskine was in his mid-twenties he had entered into correspondence with Edwards, and long after Edwards's death in 1758 he had continued to uphold Edwards's theological perspectives and to heartily recommend his books. Well described as "the paradigm of Scottish evangelical missionary interest through the last half of the eighteenth century,"[33] Erskine regularly corresponded with Ryland from

---

[31] Alan Heimert, *Religion and the American Mind: From the Great Awakening to the Revolution* (Cambridge, Massachusetts: Harvard University Press, 1966), 336.

[32] Bakke, *Power of Extraordinary Prayer*, 123.

[33] J. A. De Jong, *As the Waters Cover the Sea: Millennial Expectations in the Rise of Anglo-America Missions, 1640–1810* (Kampen, The Netherlands: J. H. Kok N.V., 1970), 166.

1780 until his death in 1803, sending him not only letters, but also, on occasion, bundles of interesting books and tracts that he sought to promote. Thus, it was in April 1784 that Erskine mailed to Ryland a copy of Edwards's *Humble Attempt*.

Reading Edwards's *Humble Attempt* in the spring of 1784 had a profound impact on Ryland, Fuller, and Sutcliff. Fuller was to preach that June at the annual meeting of the Northamptonshire Association. On his way to the meeting at Nottingham, Fuller found that heavy rains had flooded a number of spots of the roads over which he had to travel. At one particular point the flooded area appeared so deep that Fuller was reluctant to continue. A resident of the area, who knew how deep the water actually was, encouraged him to urge his horse through the water. "Go on sir," he said, "you are quite safe." As the water came up to Fuller's saddle, Fuller began to have second thoughts about continuing. "Go on, sir," the man said again, "all is right." Taking the man at his word, Fuller continued and safely traversed the flooded area of the road. This experience prompted Fuller to preach on 2 Corinthians 5:7 at the Association meeting: "We walk by faith, not by sight."[34] During the course of this sermon, which Fuller entitled, "The Nature and Importance of Walking by Faith," Fuller clearly revealed the impression Edwards's *Humble Attempt* had made upon his thinking when he appealed thus to his hearers:

> Let us take encouragement, in the present day of small things, by looking forward, and hoping for better days. Let this be attended with earnest and united prayer to Him by whom Jacob must arise. A life of faith will ever be a life of prayer. O brethren, let us pray much for an outpouring of

---

[34] *The Complete Works of the Rev. Andrew Fuller*, ed. Andrew Gunton Fuller and revised Joseph Belcher. (1845 ed.), 1:117.

God's spirit upon our ministers and churches, and not upon those only of our own connection and denomination, but upon "all that in every place call upon the name of Jesus Christ our Lord, both theirs and ours" (1 Cor. 1:2).[35]

At the same meeting Sutcliff proposed that the churches of the association establish monthly prayer meetings for the outpouring of God's Holy Spirit and the consequent revival of the churches of Great Britain. This proposal was adopted by the representatives of the 16 churches at the meeting, and on the last page of the circular letter sent out that year to the churches of the Association there was a call for them "to wrestle with God for the effusion of His Holy Spirit."[36] After recommending that there be corporate prayer for one hour on the first Monday evening of the month, the call, most likely drawn up by Sutcliff, continued:

The grand object in prayer is to be, that the Holy Spirit may be poured down on our ministers and churches, that sinners may be converted, the saints edified, the interest of religion revived, and the name of God glorified. At the same time remember, we trust you will not confine your requests to your own societies [i.e. churches] or to your own immediate connection [i.e. denomination]; let the whole interest of the Redeemer be affectionately remembered, and the spread of the gospel to the most distant parts of the habitable globe be the object of your most fervent requests. We shall rejoice if any other Christian societies of our own or other denomination will unite with us, and do now invite them most cordially to join heart and hand in the attempt.

---

[35] *Works of the Rev. Andrew Fuller*, 1:131.

[36] Attached to John Ryland, Jr., *The Nature, Evidences, and Advantages of Humility*, 12.

Who can tell what the consequences of such an united effort in prayer may be! Let us plead with God the many gracious promises of His word, which relate to the future success of His gospel. He has said, "I will yet for this be inquired of by the house of Israel, to do it for them, I will increase them with men like a flock" (Ezek. 36:37). Surely we have love enough for Zion to set apart one hour at a time, twelve times in a year, to seek her welfare.[37]

There are at least four noteworthy points about this Prayer Call. First, very much in evidence in this statement, as well as in the extract from Fuller's sermon, is the conviction that any reversal of the decline of the Calvinistic Baptists could not be accomplished by mere human zeal, but must be effected by the Spirit of God. As Sutcliff noted later in strongly Edwardsean language:

The outpouring of the divine Spirit ... is the grand promise of the New Testament.... His influences are the soul, the great animating soul of all religion. These withheld, divine ordinances are empty cisterns, and spiritual graces are withering flowers. These suspended, the greatest human abilities labour in vain, and noblest efforts fall success.[38]

Then there is the catholicity that is recommended with regard to the subjects of prayer. As the Calvinistic Baptists of the Northamptonshire Association gathered together to pray, they were encouraged not to think simply of their own churches and their own denomination, but they were to embrace in prayer believers of other denominational bodies. The kingdom of God consists of more than Calvinistic Baptists! In fact, churches of

---

[37] Ryland, Jr., *The Nature, Evidences, and Advantages of Humility*, 12.

[38] *Jealousy for the Lord of Hosts Illustrated* (London: W. Button, 1791), 12.

other associations were encouraged to join with them in praying for revival.

Third, there is the distinct missionary emphasis of the Prayer Call. The members of the Association churches were urged to pray that the gospel be spread "to the most distant parts of the habitable globe." Little did these Baptists realize how God would begin to fulfill these very prayers within the space of less than a decade.

Finally, the sole foundation for praying for revival is located in the Scriptures. Only one text, Ezekiel 36:37, is actually cited, but those issuing this call to prayer are aware of "many gracious promises" in God's Word that speak of the successful advance of His kingdom. At first glance this passage from Ezekiel hardly seems the best text to support the Prayer Call. Yet Edwards had cited this very verse in his *Humble Attempt* and said the following with regard to it:

> The Scriptures don't only direct and encourage us in general to pray for the Holy Spirit above all things else, but it is the expressly revealed will of God, that His church should be very much in prayer for that glorious outpouring of the Spirit that is to be in the latter days, and the things that shall be accomplished by it. God speaking of that blessed event (Ezek. 36), under the figure of "cleansing the house of Israel from al their iniquities, planting and building their waste and ruined places, and making them to become like the Garden of Eden, and filling them with men like a flock, like the holy flock, the flock of Jerusalem in her solemn feasts" [vv. 33-38] (wherein He doubtless has respect to the same glorious restoration and advancement of His church that is spoken of in the next chapter, and in all the following chapters to the end of the book) he says, v.37, "Thus saith the Lord, I will yet for this be inquired of by the house of Israel, to do it for them." Which doubtless implies, that it is the will of God that extraordinary prayer-

fulness of His people for this mercy should precede the be-stowment of it.[39]

Here, Edwards interprets Ezekiel 36:37 in the light of the larger context of Ezekiel 37–48. According to Edwards, since these chapters speak prophetically of the latter-day glory of the church—a millennial period in which "love will abound, and glorifying God by word and deed will be characteristic"[40]—then Ezekiel 36:37 must refer to the united prayers of God's people that will usher in this glorious period of the church's history. Edwards had directed his own congregation to "observe what you read [in the Scriptures]. Observe how things come in. Take notice of the drift of the discourse. . . ."[41] Here, in the *Humble Attempt*, he was practicing what he preached.

Now, while Edwards's particular interpretation of these passages from Ezekiel is open to debate, the principle that he draws from Ezekiel 36:37 is not; namely that preceding times of revival and striking extensions of Christ's kingdom there invariably occur the concerted and constant prayers of Christians. It is clearly this principle that those who issued the Prayer Call of 1784 wanted to stress, although most of them probably concurred with Edwards's postmillennial vision.

**The Fruit of Praying**

The Association meetings at which this Prayer Call was issued were held on June 2–3. At the end of that month, on June

---

[39] "Humble Attempt," 348.

[40] John H. Gerstner, *Jonathan Edwards: A Mini-Theology* (Wheaton, IL: Tyndale House Publishers, 1987), 96.

[41] Stephen J. Stein, "The Quest for the Spiritual Sense: The biblical Hermeneutics of Jonathan Edwards," *The Harvard Theological Review*, 70 (1977), 108.

29, the church that Sutcliff pastored in Olney resolved to establish a "monthly meeting for prayer. . .to seek for a revival of religion."[42] The passing years did not diminish Sutcliff's zeal in praying for revival and stirring up such prayer. For instance, Ryland wrote in his diary for January 21, 1788:

> Brethren Fuller, Sutcliff, [William] Carey, and I kept this day as a private fast, in my study: read the Epistles to Timothy and Titus; [Abraham] Booth's charge to [Thomas] Hopkins; [Richard] Blackerby's Life, in [John] Gillies; and [John] Rogers of Dedham's sixty Memorials for a Godly Life: and each prayed twice—Carey with singular enlargement and pungency. Our chief design was to implore a revival of godliness in our own souls, in our churches, and in the church at large.[43]

And in 1789, the number of prayer meetings for revival having grown considerably, Sutcliff decided to bring out an edition of Edwards's *Humble Attempt* to further encourage those meeting

---

[42] "Baptist Meeting at Olney Minutes", entry for June 29, 1784 (Church Minute Book, Olney, Buckinghamshire, England).

[43] Jonathan Edwards Ryland, "Memoir of Dr. Ryland" in *Pastoral Memorials: Selected from the Manuscripts of the Late Revd. John Ryland, D.D. of Bristol*, 1:17. Abraham Booth (1734-1806) was a well-known Baptist minister in London. His charge to Thomas Hopkins, when the latter was ordained pastor of Eagle Street Baptist Church, London, contains the following admonition, which would not have been lost to Sutcliff and his friends: "With humility, with prayer, and with expectation, the assistance of the holy Spirit should be daily regarded." ("Pastoral Cautions: An Address to the Late Mr. Thomas Hopkins," *The Works of Abraham Booth*, 3:178.) Richard Blackerby (1574-1648) and John Rogers (d. 1636) were both Puritan authors. The book of John Gillies (1712-1796), the son-in-law of John McLaurin, one of the initiators of the concert of prayer in Scotland, is his *Historical Collections Relating to Remarkable Periods of the Success of the Gospel, and Eminent Instruments Employed in Promoting It*. This book is reputedly the earliest history of revivals.

for prayer. Measuring only six and one quarter inches long, and three and three-quarter inches wide, and containing 168 pages, this edition was clearly designed to be a handy pocket-size edition. In his "Preface" to this edition, Sutcliff reemphasized that the Prayer Call issued by the Northamptonshire Association five years earlier was not intended for simply Calvinistic Baptists. Rather, they ardently wished it might become general among the real friends of truth and holiness.

Hard on the heels of the republication of Edwards's treatise came the events leading to the formation of the "Particular Baptist Society for the Propagation of the Gospel among the Heathen" in 1792, later known as the Baptist Missionary Society. Included among the items recommended for prayer in the Prayer Call of 1784 had been "the spread of the gospel to the most distant parts of the habitable globe." God answered their prayers in this regard in two ways: First, by providing a man with the desire to go and evangelize peoples to whom the name of Christ was completely unknown, namely William Carey (1761-1834); and, second, by giving other believers the strength and courage to support him as he went and labored.[44] Over the next four decades Carey's example would spur numerous others to offer themselves for missionary service. Of these missionary candidates, a good number would be sent to Sutcliff to be tutored by him in a parsonage seminary that he opened at the close of the 1790s.

In 1794, two years after the formation of the Baptist Missionary Society, John Rippon (1750–1836), pastor of Carter Lane Baptist Church in Southwark, London, published a list of Calvinistic Baptist congregations and ministers in his *Baptist*

---

[44] For the details, see especially Timothy George, *Faithful Witness: The Life and Mission of William Carey* (Birmingham, Alabama: New Hope, 1991).

*Annual Register*. Rippon estimated that there were at that time 326 churches in England and 56 in Wales, more than double the number that had existed in 1750.[45] He printed another list of churches four years later, according to which the numbers had grown to 361 churches in England and 84 in Wales.[46] Reflecting on these numbers Rippon wrote, "It is said that more of our meeting houses have been enlarged within the last five years, and built within the last fifteen, than had been built and enlarged for thirty years before."[47]

Rippon was not exaggerating. There was indeed steady growth among the Calvinistic Baptists during the last four decades of the eighteenth century, but it was not until the final decade of the century that there was a truly rapid influx of converts.[48] It is surely no coincidence that preceding and accompanying this growth were the concerts of prayer that many churches had established in response to the Prayer Call of 1784.

On the fiftieth anniversary of the founding of the Baptist Missionary Society, F.A. Cox, reflecting on the origins of the Society, stated that:

> The primary cause of the missionary excitement in Carey's mind, and its diffusion among the Northamptonshire ministers [was]. . .the meeting of the Association in 1784, at Nottingham, [when] it was resolved to set apart an hour on the first Monday evening of every month, "for extraordinary prayer for revival of religion, and for the extending of Christ's kingdom in the world." This suggestion proceeded

---

[45] *The Baptist Annual Register* (London, 1797), 2:16, 23.

[46] *The Baptist Annual Register* (London, 1801), 3:40, 42.

[47] *Baptist Annual Register*, 3:40.

[48] Deryck W. Lovegrove, *Established Church, Sectarian People: Itineracy and the Transformation of English Dissent, 1780-1830* (Cambridge: Cambridge University Press, 1988), 38.

from the venerable Sutcliff. Its simplicity and appropriate-
ness have since recommended it to universal adoption; and
copious showers of blessing from on high have been
poured forth upon the churches.[49]

From the vantage point of the early 1840s, Cox saw the
Prayer Call of 1784 as pivotal in that it focused the prayers of
Calvinistic Baptist churches in the Northamptonshire Association on the nations of the world, and thus prepared the way for
the emergence of the Baptist Missionary Society and the sending
of Carey to India. Yet he also notes that the "universal adoption" of the concert of prayer by churches beyond the ranks of
the Calvinistic Baptist denomination had led to rich times of
revival, when God poured forth upon these churches "copious
showers of blessing." Later historians would describe this period
of blessing as the Second Evangelical Awakening (1790-1830).
Some of them, like J. Edwin Orr and Paul E.G. Cook, would
concur with Cox and rightly trace the human origins of this
time of revival and spiritual awakening to the adoption of the
concert of prayer by the Calvinistic Baptists in 1784.[50]

However, in one area Cox's statement is somewhat mislead-
ing. In describing Sutcliff as "the venerable Sutcliff" he leaves
the reader with an idyllic impression of the Baptist pastor. How
sobering to find that this man, who was at the heart of a prayer
movement that God used to bring so much spiritual blessing to
His church, also struggled when it came to prayer. When Sutcliff lay dying in 1814 he said to Fuller, "I wish I had prayed

----

[49] *History of the Baptist Missionary Society, From 1792 to 1842* (London: T.
Ward & Co./G. & J. Dyer, 1842), 1:10-11.

[50] J. Edwin Orr, *The Eager Feet: Evangelical Awakenings 1790-1830* (Chicago:
Moody Press, 1975), 95, 191-92, 199; Paul E. G. Cook, "The Forgotten Revival" in *Preaching and Revival* (London: The Westminster Conference, 1984),
92.

more."[51] For some time Fuller ruminated on this statement by his dying friend. Eventually he came to the conviction that Sutcliff did not mean that he "wished he had prayed more frequently, but more *spiritually*." Then Fuller elaborated on this interpretation by applying Sutcliff's statement to his own life:

> I wish I had prayed more for the influence of the Holy Spirit; I might have enjoyed more of the power of vital godliness. I wish I had prayed more for the assistance of the Holy Spirit, in studying and preaching my sermons; I might have seen more of the blessing of God attending my ministry. I wish I had prayed more for the outpouring of the Holy Spirit to attend the labours of our friends in India; I might have witnessed more of the effects of their efforts in the conversion of the heathen.[52]

---

[51] Fuller, "Principles and Prospects," in *Works of the Rev. Andrew Fuller*, 1:344.

[52] J. W. Morris, *Memoirs of the Life and Writings of the Rev. Andrew Fuller* (London, 1816), 443.

# Effectual, Fervent Prayer
## Phil Johnson

"The prayer of a righteous person has great power as it is working. Elijah was a man with a nature like ours, and he prayed fervently that it might not rain, and for three years and six months it did not rain on the earth. Then he prayed again, and heaven gave rain, and the earth bore its fruit." (James 5:16-18, NASB)

One clear lesson about prayer that permeates almost every biblical passage on the subject of prayer is the promise that God answers the fervent prayer of a righteous man. When we ask in faith, God answers. That's the same promise Jesus made in Matthew 21:22: "Whatever you ask in prayer, you will receive, if you have faith." Mark 11:24: "Whatever you ask in prayer, believe that you have received it, and it will be yours." And "this is the confidence that we have toward Him, that if we ask anything according to His will He hears us. And if we know that He hears us in whatever we ask, we know that we have the requests that we have asked of Him" (1 John 5:14-15).

Those, of course, are not promises that we can manipulate God with our praying. The promise of answered prayer doesn't function as some kind of exception clause to the doctrine of divine sovereignty. Notice the qualifying phrase in that text from 1 John: "If we ask any thing *according to His will*, He hears us."

True faith is confidence in the power and the promises of God. Authentic faith is not an expression of self-will. Nor is it merely positive thinking—as if we could get God to do what we want simply by convincing ourselves that we'll get what we want if we think hard enough and positively enough about it. That's what most of the charlatans on religious television teach, and they sometimes quote Mark 11:24: "Whatever you ask in prayer, believe that you have received it, and it will be yours." But what they are really peddling is nothing less than blind gullibility and sinful presumption masquerading as religious belief. It is certainly not what Jesus meant when He spoke about the prayer of faith.

Genuine faith is grounded in God's promises and a true understanding of God's will. If you think God is going to grant a prayer request that is inconsistent with His character; if you imagine that He is going to do something that contradicts His promises; if you delude yourself into thinking He will give you anything that is contrary to His Word; or if you think He's going to say "yes" to a prayer request that is in conflict with His will—it doesn't matter how much you have managed to convince yourself to believe in what you are praying for, that is not faith; it is sheer *effrontery*.

Those who pray like that are also guilty of praying selfishly. And in James 4:3 we are told that selfish prayers go unanswered: "You ask and do not receive, because you ask wrongly, to spend it on your passions."

So when Jesus tells us to pray in faith and not to doubt, that's not a lesson about the power of "positive confession." Scripture does not encourage us to cultivate blind confidence that we can have whatever we desire. These promises ought to encourage us to understand the will of God and ground our praying (and our faith) not in our own selfish desires, but in the certainty of God's promises, and in the steadfast faithfulness of His righteous character. Have *faith*, not presumption, when you pray.

But let's not obscure James 5:16 in a mist of negative qualifications. There is a very positive and encouraging principle in this text: When a righteous person prays earnestly and fervently, it avails much; it is of great benefit. That is first and foremost an encouragement to be faithful and fervent in our praying. It's a promise that we are not wasting time when we pray.

And the person James holds up to us as a flesh-and-blood example of this is Elijah. If you study the life and ministry of Elijah, one of the things that stands out about him is the fact that he prayed at every crisis point in his ministry. And God *always* answered his prayers.

James says that you and I can expect the same thing in our experience if our praying is fervent and faithful, if we persist in prayer, and if we pray according to the will of God rather than out of selfish motives.

After all, James says, "Elijah was a man with a nature like ours." Elijah wasn't supernatural. He was a spiritual hero, but not some kind of *super*hero. He was a fallen human being, just like you and me, subject to the same passions and fears and fits of depression. Scripture records his failures as well as his triumphs.

But he was a *righteous* man, despite his sin, because he was justified by faith. He trusted God, and therefore righteousness was imputed to him. That's what James means when he speaks of "a righteous person" in verse 16. He's talking about believers, those who are clothed in the perfect righteousness of Christ.

Verse 17 says: "Elijah was a man with a nature like ours, and he prayed fervently that it might not rain, and for three years and six months it did not rain on the earth." It's interesting that there is no record of that prayer in the Old Testament. Elijah first appears on the scene in 1 Kings 17:1, and simply announces to King Ahab, in Ahab's own court, that there would not be dew nor rain in Israel until he (Elijah) gave the word.

James, writing under the inspiration of the Holy Spirit, informs us that the drought was a response to Elijah's fervent prayer. Those three and a half years brought the whole nation to its knees, and Elijah became known as the troubler of Israel. Then, finally, when it was time to end the drought, James 5:18 says: "He prayed again, and heaven gave rain, and the earth bore its fruit."

I'm intrigued by the nature of Elijah's second prayer, the details of which James does not go into. But it's noteworthy that the drought-ending prayer *is* recorded for us in the Old Testament. In fact, in 1 Kings 18, there's a detailed account of how the drought ended. It shows Elijah's persistence in prayer, his boldness, and his faith. It is well worth examining that prayer with care.

The prayer in question comes immediately after Elijah's famous victory over the prophets of Baal on Mt. Carmel. Elijah had called down fire from heaven, humiliated the Baal-priests publicly, and then ordered them to be slaughtered as a judgment for the evil they had done by corrupting Israel with pagan worship. That was Elijah's greatest moment of public triumph ever. It is one of the most memorable moments of triumph in the entire Old Testament.

But public accolades were not what Elijah was seeking. His mission was to vindicate Jehovah, not to magnify himself, and Elijah's greatest work on Carmel was not yet complete. He had come to Mt. Carmel not merely to call down fire from heaven, but more importantly to call down rain. He had completely triumphed over the false prophets of Baal, but the full public vindication of Jehovah was not yet complete—and would not be complete until God opened the heavens again.

There's a fascinating contrast between how Elijah called down the fire and how he called down the rain. He had called down fire in the most public way, with a simple, audible petition to the Lord before all the people. The prayer for fire consists of just two verses of Scripture: "O LORD, God of Abraham, Isaac, and Israel, let it be known this day that you are God in Israel, and that I am your servant, and that I have done all these things at your word. Answer me, O LORD, answer me, that this people may know that you, O LORD, are God, and that you have turned their hearts back" (1 Kings 18:36-37). There was no dramatic pleading. In fact, Elijah did not even mention fire. The heart of the prayer is really a plea for the repentance of Israel. The simplicity and calm quietness of Elijah's prayer made a stark contrast to all the screaming and writhing and bloody flesh-cutting that the priests of Baal had exhibited when they were trying in vain to get *their* god to answer (vv. 26-29).

God answered Elijah's prayer for fire instantly, apparently without delay, and in the most dramatic fashion, sending a fire so hot that it evaporated several barrels of sea water with which Elijah had drenched his offering. It was a spectacular demonstration of *God's* power, in response to the earnest prayer of a single righteous man.

You might think Elijah would call down the rain in a similar fashion, but that is not what happened. In the scene that follows the slaughter of the prophets, Elijah went up on Carmel alone with one of his servants and pleaded again and again for rain. This time he went away from the crowd to pray. This time the answer didn't come so immediately or so dramatically. In fact, when the answer *did* come, it appeared in the most insignificant way—with the advent of a tiny cloud so far away on the horizon that its appearance probably would have been enough to discourage most of us.

But follow the story to the end, and the rain finally does fall in a way that is at least as dramatic as the falling of the fire, proving that God is certainly no less powerful in the bestowing of His blessings than He is in the dispensing of His judgments.

And the whole episode reminds us that God's blessings are reserved for those who pursue His promises with a patient and tenacious faith.

The effectual, fervent prayer of a righteous man can sometimes seem like hard and discouraging work.

This episode is a great lesson about how to pray rightly. Here is the pertinent section of Scripture—1 Kings 18:41–46. (This is what ensued immediately after Elijah ordered the slaughter of the Baal-priests):

> And Elijah said to Ahab, "Go up, eat and drink, for there is a sound of the rushing of rain." So Ahab went up to eat and to drink. And Elijah went up to the top of Mount Carmel. And he bowed himself down on the earth and put his face between his knees. And he said to his servant, "Go up now, look toward the sea." And he went up and looked and said, "There is nothing." And he said, "Go again," seven times. And at the seventh time he said, "Behold, a little cloud like a man's hand is rising from the sea." And he said, "Go up, say to Ahab, 'Prepare your chariot and go down, lest the rain stop you.'" And in a little while the heavens grew black with clouds and wind, and there was a great rain. And Ahab rode and went to Jezreel. And the hand of the LORD was on Elijah, and he gathered up his garment and ran before Ahab to the entrance of Jezreel.

Three characteristics of Elijah's prayer are worth paying careful attention to. These features characterize how all of us should pray. They're the very features Jesus stressed when He taught His disciples to pray. Notice how they all underscore the beautiful sincerity and simplicity of righteous praying.

### Elijah Prayed Privately

By the time we get to this point in the biblical account of Elijah's life, Scripture has already recorded some remarkable instances of Elijah's praying, with miraculous answers to his prayers. In 1 Kings 17 he prayed that God would restore life to the dead son of the widow of Zarephath, and the Lord raised that little boy up. Then, of course, in the early part of this scene in 1 Kings 18, Elijah had prayed for fire from heaven, and the fire instantly fell and consumed his sacrifice in the sight of all Israel. We also know from James, of course, that Elijah had prayed for the drought in the first place. So we know that the Lord has already answered three of Elijah's prayers with amazing miracles.

The prayer for fire from heaven was the only one of those prayers that was prayed in public. The others are private prayers. And even now, at the height of his victory on Mt. Carmel, when a lesser man would want to bask in the amazement of the crowd and savor the public aspect of his victory, Elijah retreats to pray to the Lord in private.

I love the way Elijah simply dismisses Ahab (v. 41): "Go up, eat and drink, for there is a sound of the rushing of rain." Here you see something of the contrasting characters of Elijah and Ahab. Elijah had come alone to Mt. Carmel. Ahab apparently had prepared and brought some kind of feast and a large entourage along with him, no doubt fully expecting that he would be celebrating the demise of his most hated enemy.

The size of the crowd Ahab brought with him is a reflection of his gargantuan ego. To start with, he had brought 450 of Jezebel's prophets. He had apparently also brought a number of people from the royal court, royal servants, tents, a movable feast—everything he needed to have a royal celebration on one of the plateaus of Mt. Carmel as soon as the showdown was over. The only person who seems to have been missing from the retinue was Ahab's evil wife, Jezebel. For reasons that Scripture does not explain, she was not there on Mt. Carmel, and that is why (according to 1 Kings 19:1) Ahab had to report to her what had happened when he got back to Jezreel.

Ahab was apparently not quite the sort of fanatical Baal-worshiper his wife was. He doesn't seem to have been a religious man at all. He tolerated and to some degree participated in Jezebel's evil religious practices, but it was Jezebel, not Ahab, whose commitment to Baal set the spiritual standard for Ahab's regime. She was the wicked force behind the paganism in Israel during the years of Ahab's reign. 1 Kings 21:25 says: "There was none who sold himself to do what was evil in the sight of the LORD like Ahab, whom Jezebel his wife incited [urged on; stirred up]." Notice that according to 1 Kings 19:2 it was *Jezebel* who went into a rage when she heard about the slaughter of the prophets. Ahab was there on Mt. Carmel when it occurred, and he couldn't stop it. In fact, he comes across like someone who was afraid of Elijah.

Everything Scripture tells us about him suggests that Ahab was a weak man, utterly lacking in character and convictions. He was undoubtedly intimidated when the crowd's mood turned against him and people suddenly fell on their faces, shouting "The LORD, he is God; the LORD, he is God" (v. 39). So Ahab would naturally have been reluctant to try to intervene when the mob started rounding up the Baal-prophets to behead them.

But even if craven fear was the main thing that kept him silent on Mt. Carmel, he still does not seem to have regarded the killing of the Baal-priests as a *personal* loss the way Jezebel did. It didn't inflame his passions the way it inflamed hers. They weren't Ahab's Baal-priests; it wasn't his religion—all of that was a reflection of Jezebel's obsession.

In fact, after it was all over, he seems to have been eager to get on with his banquet anyway, and Elijah sensed that. So there's probably a tone of utter contempt and indignation in Elijah's voice when he says to Ahab, "Go, eat and drink."

There's also an amazing attitude of *authority* in Elijah's words. He was dismissing Ahab from his presence. He wanted to be alone with God, and at this moment Ahab was an unwanted distraction. Elijah clearly wanted to be rid of his presence.

Ahab may have been relieved just to get away with his life. He also now had a promise from Elijah that the three-and-a-half-year drought would soon end, and rain would be abundant once more. Beyond that, there was not a lot for Ahab to celebrate because he had to go home and tell his wife that all her priests had been defeated and killed because of one solitary man. But Ahab was not going to miss the opportunity for a feast. So he went to the plateau where his tents were pitched and his banquet was ready. Verse 42 says: "So Ahab went up to eat and to drink. And Elijah went up to the top of Mount Carmel. And he bowed himself down on the earth and put his face between his knees." Going up to the very pinnacle of Carmel, where he could be alone with God, Elijah began to pray for rain. He prayed silently, or perhaps in a hushed tone that was between him and God alone. Both Elijah's posture and the fact that Scripture doesn't record the actual words of his prayer underscore the quiet intimacy of his communion with God.

Elijah had already won his *public* victory. Jehovah had been vindicated before all Israel, and the Baal-priests had paid for their false prophecies with their lives. That was perfectly in accord with the penalty spelled out in Moses' law. Elijah *could* have indulged himself with the congratulations of the crowd. He might well have felt the temptation to revel in a popularity that he had never known before. Had he been like some religious celebrities in our time, he would have milked this moment of triumph for its public relations value, seized the opportunity to gain a popular following, and set himself up with political power and public recognition so that he would never again have to live in hiding and suffer the lack of material blessings he had endured for the previous three and a half years.

But Elijah shunned all of that, and at the first opportunity he got alone with God again so he could pray in quiet.

This is in perfect harmony with what Jesus taught in the Sermon on the Mount: "When you pray, you must not be like the hypocrites. For they love to stand and pray in the synagogues and at the street corners, that they may be seen by others. Truly, I say to you, they have received their reward. But when you pray, go into your room and shut the door and pray to your Father who is in secret. And your Father who sees in secret will reward you" (Matthew 6:5–6). If we're going to commune meaningfully with God, it is ultimately necessary to shut ourselves off from the commotion and ungodliness of this world, and get alone to seek Him in private prayer. Elijah sensed that need even in the midst of his most public victory.

### Elijah Prayed Passionately

Here's a second feature of Elijah's prayer worth pointing out: Notice how he assumes the most abject posture before the Lord, not merely kneeling, but also putting his face to the ground between his knees.

When Elijah confronted the people of Israel—even when he was in the presence of Ahab—he stood resolutely, unbendingly, strong and erect before them. He was no wimp. He wasn't a weakling who bowed before any man.

But when he went before God in prayer, he bowed as low as his frame would permit him to bow. He has done this before. In fact, when he prayed for the widow's dead son in 1 Kings 17:21, he stretched himself out prostrate on the boy's dead body.

Elijah's bowing posture reflects, first of all, his deep reverence for God. This is a concept that is all too often lost in this worldly and impious generation. The typical Christian today approaches God with far too much familiarity and far too little fear. It's a sad fact that the very word *reverence* has an old-fashioned ring to us. The typical Christian today would tell you that he feels more spiritually refreshed and invigorated by the high-fiving enthusiasm of a stadium rally than he does by an hour alone with God in prayer. And that fact alone speaks volumes about the spiritual state of the church.

But I think Elijah's posture suggests something in addition to his fear of the Lord. He wasn't merely showing his reverence by taking this posture. It *was* that; it *was* a posture of abject humility and meekness. But it also reveals his deep passion. The expression used in the King James Version of verse 42 captures a sense of the verb that may not be conveyed in other translations: "He *cast* himself down upon the earth." He physically threw himself on his face before God. There's an intensity in the expression that tells us this was a prayer of great passion.

Elijah, along with everyone else in Israel, had endured three and a half long years of drought. The whole nation had been strained to the breaking point by the impact of that drought. Everyone thirsted for relief, but no one longed for refreshment more than Elijah.

Elijah saw the spiritual significance of the drought. He knew it was a judgment of God against the nation for their apostasy. The drought was the fulfillment of a warning Moses had given Israel when they left Egypt. The Lord was bringing them into a land of milk and honey. Here is how Deuteronomy 8:7-9 describes the Promised Land:

> For the LORD your God is bringing you into a good land, a land of brooks of water, of fountains and springs, flowing out in the valleys and hills, a land of wheat and barley, of vines and fig trees and pomegranates, a land of olive trees and honey, a land in which you will eat bread without

scarcity, in which you will lack nothing, a land whose
stones are iron, and out of whose hills you can dig copper.

But Deuteronomy 28 prophesied what would happen if the
people turned away from the Lord: "The heavens over your
head shall be bronze, and the earth under you shall be iron. The
LORD will make the rain of your land powder. From heaven
dust shall come down on you until you are destroyed"
(Deuteronomy 28:23-24).

The earth as iron pictures the hardness of the soil after a
long period without rain, and the heavens as brass may suggest
the constant shining of the sun. But the imagery of heaven as
brass also suggests the utter silence and impenetrability of
heaven. It was as if a brass shield had been put in place so that
prayers for rain would not reach the throne of God.

What Moses prophesied is exactly what had occurred in
Elijah's day. The earth was as iron and the heavens had become
as brass. The curse of God was over all the land. The drought
signified the spiritual dryness of Israel, and the rains would not
come until the people turned to the Lord again.

Now, in the wake of Elijah's victory on Mt. Carmel, the
people had to some degree recanted Baal worship. And by
killing the priests they had begun to put the evil away from
themselves. History suggests this was neither widespread nor
complete repentance, but it was a token of the right response,
and Elijah knew it was time for the Lord to open the heavens.
He longed to see that happen. So he prayed with fervent
passion.

### Elijah Prayed Persistently

Elijah's private, passionate praying was also persistent. He
had a promise from God that it would rain again. This chapter
in his story began when "the word of the LORD came to Elijah,

in the third year, saying, 'Go, show yourself to Ahab, and I will send rain upon the earth' " (1 Kings 18:1).

Some people might think such a promise would mean Elijah didn't *need* to pray. After all, he had an iron-clad promise from God! Why should he have to pray for what the Lord had already promised?

But Elijah did not think that way, and neither should we. It is true that He is faithful who promises, but along with His promises He commands us to pray without ceasing.

That may seem like a paradox to the natural mind, but it is clearly what Scripture teaches. Remember, it was Jesus who said, "Do not be anxious about your life, what you will eat or what you will drink, nor about your body, what you will put on" (Matthew 6:25). He went on (vv. 31–34):

> Do not be anxious, saying, "What shall we eat?" or "What shall we drink?" or "What shall we wear?" For the Gentiles seek after all these things, and your heavenly Father knows that you need them all. But seek first the kingdom of God and his righteousness, and all these things will be added to you. Therefore do not be anxious about tomorrow, for tomorrow will be anxious for itself. Sufficient for the day is its own trouble.

That's a promise to each of us that God knows our daily needs and promises to supply our food and clothing. It is a sin to fret about such things. God has *promised* we will not lack them.

And yet when Jesus taught His disciples to pray, He instructed them to pray, "Give us this day our daily bread." Just because God has made a promise does not mean we should not pray for what He promised.

God gives His promises to stir our hearts to prayer, not to keep us from having to pray. God's promises teach us what we are to pray for. In the words of F. B. Meyer, the promises are "the mould into which we may pour our fervid spirits without fear. They are the signed cheque, made payable to order, which we must endorse and present for payment."[1] Arthur Pink commented on the same principle. He points out that "In Ezekiel 36:24–36 will be found a whole string of promises, yet in immediate connection [with those promises] we read [where God says], 'I will yet for this *be inquired of* by the house of Israel, *to do it* for them,' v. 37."[2]

I sometimes hear Christians complain that God does not seem to fulfill His promises for them. They can't find peace, or they seem to have needs that are going unmet, or they are frustrated spiritually, continually falling into the same sins, and even though God promises a way of escape from temptation, they can't seem to find the way of escape. If that is where you find yourself spiritually, let me remind you of James 4:2: "You do not have, because you do not ask." Just because God has promised something does not mean you don't need to pray for it.

Elijah had the promise of rain. But that did not stop him from praying fervently for the fulfillment of the promise. With his heart emboldened by that promise, he began to beseech the Lord to send the rain. From the top of Mount Carmel, where he had a good view of all sides, he went down on his knees and, placing his head between those knees, he earnestly prayed for rain.

We cannot explain why the rain did not fall instantly, in the same manner the fire had fallen earlier. All we can do is take note that God sometimes answers us quickly, and sometimes He

---

[1] *Elijah and the Secret of His Power* (Ft. Washington, PA: Christian Literature Crusade, 1972 reprint), 77–78.

**2** *Elijah* (Edinburgh: Banner of Truth, 1956), 184.

makes us wait. Even a prophet like Elijah was not always answered *immediately*. Who are we to think God should always answer our prayers without delay?

But we can be certain that God's delays always have good reasons. We may never see what those reasons are, but we know the character of God, and we know that He is good, and merciful, and all his ways are right. His time is the *best* time. He makes all things "beautiful in His time" (Ecclesiastes 3:11). He does not delay just to toy with us. He's not playing tyrannical games when He withholds the fulfillment of His promises for a time. But Scripture assures us that even His delays are always tokens of His grace and mercy to us.

Often, when the Lord waits, it is so that He can pour out the answer in a superabundant way. Elijah prayed for rain, and when the answer did not come immediately he persisted. What he ultimately received was a torrential downpour—exceedingly, abundantly above what he could ask or think.

It is also true that often when the Lord waits it is so that we can mature and learn about Him in the waiting process. We must wait for *His* time, because His time is always right.

Whatever the reasons, it is always for our good that He waits, so that our faith can be strengthened, so that we can benefit from the greater abundance of His blessings, and so that, when the answer finally does come, we will receive it with more gratitude and see His hand more clearly in the answer.

Notice what happened in Elijah's case: He had a servant, possibly a youth or a young boy. The servant might have even been the son of the widow of Zarephath, whom Elijah had recently raised from the dead. And as Elijah prayed for rain, he sent the servant to a place high on the mountain summit where he had a view of the Mediterranean ocean. And he told the servant (v. 43), "Go up now, look toward the sea."

The servant went and looked, but the sky was as dry and clear as it had been for almost 4 years. So he came back to where Elijah was praying and said, "There is nothing" (v. 43). And Elijah said, "Go again." And after a little while longer the servant came back and said, "There is nothing." And Elijah said, "Go again." And he came back a third time and said, "There is nothing." And Elijah said, "Go again."

Meanwhile, Elijah kept praying. We don't know how long all this took, but it must have been a considerable time—hours, not minutes. And no doubt each time the servant went, he would stay a little longer, but then he would finally get discouraged, and again come back to Elijah, saying, "There is nothing." And Elijah would say, "Go again." And that happened *seven times!*

I don't think Elijah was discouraged. He had experience with this kind of delayed reply. When he raised the young boy from the dead, the answer to *that* prayer did not come immediately. He had to pray three times. But here the delay is more than doubled. Yet there's no peep of protest or sigh of discouragement from Elijah. He simply kept praying. He had a promise from God, and he *knew* the answer would come in time.

In fact, notice Elijah's words to Ahab when he sent him away (v. 41): "Elijah said to Ahab, 'Go up, eat and drink, for there is a sound of the rushing of rain.'" What do you think Elijah meant by that? It is clear that there was no visible rain storm yet on the horizon, so there could not have been any actual sound of rain. The top of Mt. Carmel is 1742 feet above sea level and barely 13 miles inland from the Mediterranean coast. From there on a clear day you can see more than a hundred miles over the horizon, and Elijah's servant saw nothing, as far as he could see in every direction. That means when Elijah said these words to Ahab, there was not a storm cell within a hundred miles of them. There is no way Elijah could literally hear with his physical ears the actual sound of rain.

But so certain was he of the promise of God that Elijah could hear with the ears of faith what he was certain was about to occur. The heavens were about to let loose with a torrent the likes of which Ahab could scarcely imagine. Elijah didn't literally hear the sound of an approaching storm, but by faith he knew one was coming.

And that is why Elijah did not grow discouraged or weary while praying and seeing no tangible sign of an answer. He endured as seeing that which is invisible. He remained steadfast, hearing that which is inaudible. By faith he persisted, because he knew the faithfulness of God; he had seen God answer before, and he knew that the answer would come in God's time.

This kind of thing was a recurring theme in the life of Elijah. God always seemed to take the prophet to the very brink before He finally answered his prayers. First, He placed Elijah beside a drying brook, and didn't even tell him what the next step of the journey would be until the brook was completely dry.

Then He sent him to hide in the home of a starving widow, and supplied just enough oil and flour on a daily basis to meet their daily needs, without a speck of provisions beyond what they need.

Then the widow's son inexplicably fell sick and suddenly died, and Elijah had to pray repeatedly before the Lord revived the boy. Always the Lord's intervention in Elijah's life was at the last possible moment, and Elijah seemed to live the first half of his life constantly on the very brink of total ruin. But all of that only strengthened his faith, and made him so much more effective as a prophet. Rather than resenting it as many of us would, Elijah seemed to be enlivened and emboldened and excited by it. He drew power from the knowledge that God would work in His time and in His way—because by now Elijah could see that God's timing was always just right and His ways were always absolutely perfect.

So he calmly kept sending the impatient servant back to the edge of Mt. Carmel's summit, until on the seventh time the servant returned and said, "Behold, a little cloud like a man's hand is rising from the sea."

I gather he meant it was *shaped* like a man's hand, although it may have also been a reference to the small size of the cloud. The servant seems to have been utterly discouraged at that point, and that may have been his way of conveying his discouragement to Elijah. Finally, he spotted something on the horizon, but it was small—infinitesimally small for a cloud—and certainly no reason to rejoice.

But Elijah, man of faith that he was, saw it differently and knew that it was the answer to his prayer. So he sent the servant immediately with a message for Ahab (v. 44): "Go up, say to Ahab, 'Prepare your chariot and go down, lest the rain stop you.'" And as the breathless servant reached Ahab with the message, Ahab knew by now that Elijah's prophecies were not to be trifled with. So he harnessed his horses to the chariot, mounted the chariot, and set out for Jezreel.

Meanwhile that little cloud was gathering moisture. Verse 45 says: "And in a little while the heavens grew black with clouds and wind, and there was a great rain. And Ahab rode and went to Jezreel." Soon the heavens were literally black with roiling clouds, and those clouds unleashed a torrent of rain and wind like Israel had not seen in years.

Indeed, "The prayer of a righteous person has great power as it is working." That is certainly a strong argument for persistent prayer. We should not grow weary in praying because prayer is powerful from the moment we start praying—even when it seems like God is delaying His answer. And often an answer to prayer that follows one of God's delays is almost always a more abundant answer than those answers that come quickly.

That was certainly the case here. The heavens unleashed a flood.

It's at least 20 miles from the summit of Mt. Carmel to Jezreel, so what occurred next is nothing short of miraculous. Verse 46: "And the hand of the LORD was on Elijah, and he gathered up his garment and ran before Ahab to the entrance of Jezreel."

In a desert climate like that, when after a long period without rain, when the heavens suddenly open, the terrain very quickly turns into a cascade of swiftly-flowing mud. So it's no wonder it took Ahab and his chariot a long time to get home. But for Elijah to pass him on foot is nothing short of miraculous.

Imagine the impression that made on Ahab! In his utterly pagan mind he must have been thinking that Elijah was some kind of god himself. In fact, after this episode, whenever Ahab encountered Elijah, Scripture portrays him as trembling and fainthearted.

So this episode gives us a terrifying insight into the heart of Ahab in this account. Notice that he had no doubt whatsoever about whether Elijah's words were true. When Elijah told him it was going to rain, he knew he had better saddle up immediately and get home! He also had no doubt about Elijah's credentials. He had repeatedly seen the prophet do supernatural things. He knew these signs and wonders verified the claims of Elijah and were enabled by the infinite wisdom and almighty power of Jehovah. Yet Ahab remained as stubborn and hard-hearted as ever in his hatred of Elijah and the God he represented. He was convinced but not converted. He was actually now in a worse state than if he had never witnessed Elijah's miracles.

Still, "the prayer of a righteous person has great power as it is working."

Here's what James is saying: Your prayer life ought to be the most exciting and exhilarating aspect of your spiritual life. If you're not seeing answers to your prayers, it's not because there's something wrong with God. The problem is with your own prayer life. "You do not have, because you do not ask. You ask and do not receive, because you ask wrongly, to spend it on your passions."

Learn to pray passionately, persistently, according to the will of God, and the Word of God guarantees that your prayers will avail *much*.

# Prayer as Our Battle Cry
## R. Bruce Bickel

"Your kingdom come, your will be done,
on earth as it is in heaven." Matthew 6:10 (ESV)

Throughout history, individuals and nations at war have had a "battle cry" that would serve as a rallying point to remind the soldiers of their need to press on to victory and summon all their inner strength to fulfill the mission at hand. During the Scottish fight for independence, the Scots rallied around the phrase, "Wallace, Wallace, Wallace" (referring to their hero William Wallace). The Texans cried, "Remember the Alamo," as they fought the Mexicans under General Santa Ana. In World War II, "Remember Pearl Harbor" was all the American troops needed as a motivational reminder to continue the quest for victory in the Pacific. The Church, the Body of Christ, was given a battle cry when our Lord, in teaching us the manner, method, and matters of which we are to pray, said, ". . .Your kingdom come. . . ."(ESV). The idea of the Body of Christ being at war and the need for a "Battle Cry" is not popular in the Church today, yet the Scripture is very clear in its threefold description of God's people by using the terms remnant, persecution, and warfare. Paul certainly understood the environment in which we are engaged as a war (2 Corinthians 10:4; 1 Timothy 1:18–19). But how does this phrase "Your kingdom come" serve the Church as our "Battle Cry"?

The second petition is the briefest and yet the most comprehensive one contained in our Lord's Prayer, hereafter referred to as "The Disciples' Prayer." It is strange and sad that, in

most circles, it is the least understood. To aid us in our understanding of the significance of this petition, let us consider the
following questions: What is the relationship between this petition and the one preceding it, "Hallowed be Your name"?
Whose Kingdom is here in view? What specifically is meant by
the words, "Your Kingdom"? And, lastly, how are we to understand the words, "Your Kingdom come"?

The first petition, "Hallowed be Your name," concerns
God's glory itself, whereas the following two, "Your kingdom
come, your will be done," deal with the *means* whereby His glory
is to be made visible and promoted on earth. God's name (actually His names) stands for God Himself, revealing His nature,
character, and attributes as revealed in creation and the Scripture, and is glorified on earth only to the degree in which His
Kingdom comes to us and His will is done by us. The relationship between this petition and the first one, then, is quite obvious. First, Christ teaches us to pray for the hallowing (sanctifying) of God's great name; then He directs us to pray subsequently for the means of how that happens. There are numerous ways in which God's name is glorified, but none promotes
His glory as the coming of His Kingdom. Therefore, we are instructed in the same chapter, "But seek first the Kingdom of
God and His righteousness. . ." (Matthew 6:33 ESV). While we
should glorify God's name upon earth, we are unable to do so
in and of ourselves. God's Kingdom must first be established in
our hearts (John 3:3-8). We cannot honor God until we have
the desire to honor God, and then submit to His rule over us.

God's Kingdom comes progressively to individuals in the
following sequence and degrees: (1) God gives to men the out-
ward means of salvation by the universal gospel call (Romans
10:13-17); (2) the preached Word enters the mind, so that the
mysteries of the gospel are understood (Matthew 13:23; He-

brews 6:4-6; 10:32); (3) the Holy Spirit regenerates men, replaces their dead heart of stone with a live heart of flesh so that they enter the Kingdom of God as willing subjects of His gracious reign (John 1:12, 13; 3:3, 5: Ezekiel 36:22-27); (4) at death, the spirits of the redeemed are freed from the presence of sin (glorification) (Romans 7:24, 25; Hebrews 12:23); and (5) at the resurrection, the redeemed shall be fully glorified (Romans 8:23).

This second petition concerns God's sovereign rule, but it is not a reference to the exercising of God's universal sovereignty, as that is always in place. That has existed and continued from the beginning (Genesis 1:1). The Kingdom must, then, be future in the sense that God's reign of grace is to be consummated in the eternal glory of His Kingdom in the new heavens and new earth (2 Peter 3:13). So, what kingdom do we mean when we pray this petition? There is a twofold kingdom that is meant in these words—the kingdom of grace and the kingdom of glory. First, there is the kingdom of grace which God exercises in the consciences of the remnant (see above paragraph). The kingdom of grace is a reference to God's saving work that is not only in one sense present, but also in another sense future as it awaits a future consummation.

We must remember that we are in the kingdom of darkness (Colossians 1:13-14). By praying "Your kingdom come" we are pleading to be brought out of the domain of darkness, and that the devil's kingdom in this world will be destroyed. It is a "Battle Cry" because we are at war (Ephesians 6:11-13). We are praying that the kingdom of grace may be set up in our hearts and will increase during our lifetime. We are praying that God's saving reign—the kingdom of grace—will be expanded now, and, much more, that He will usher in the final kingdom inaugurated by Jesus' glorious return.

Second, our "Battle Cry" means that we are praying that the kingdom of glory may hasten, and that we will be translated into it in God's timing. The kingdoms of grace and glory do not differ specifically but gradually; they differ not in nature but in degree. The kingdom of grace is the first stage of the beginning of the kingdom of glory. "The kingdom of grace is glory in the seed, and the kingdom of glory is grace in the flower" (Richard Sibbes). The kingdom of grace is the beginning and the kingdom of glory is the completion. Because the connection between the kingdom of grace and the kingdom of glory is so inseparable there can be no entrance into the one but by the other. Grace leads to glory, and there can be no glory without grace. One cannot enter the kingdom of glory except through the kingdom of grace. The kingdom of grace leads to the kingdom of glory. These two God has joined together; let us not separate them.

Our "Battle Cry" has tremendous rallying implications. First, we are asking God to increase the external influence of His grace here on earth. Because we are at war we are praying that the gospel be preached and that the power of the Holy Spirit will empower it. It means we desire that the Church be strengthened and that the cause of hallowing God's name on earth be advanced and the works of Satan be destroyed. We are engaged in a spiritual battle. Second, it applies to God's internal kingdom, that is, His spiritual reign of grace within the hearts of men. We are praying that His sovereign rule will be established in our hearts, and that we desire that by our obedience to His laws His name will be magnified by our lives. Third, it applies to God's kingdom in its future glory. We are praying that the day of our Lord's return will come quickly so that Satan and his army shall be completely vanquished and God's people shall be done with sinning forever. Last, by praying this "Battle Cry", we are affirming that we have surrendered the rule of our own life and are asking the Holy Spirit to take control for His glory.

We have been taught to determine our own destiny by charting our own course and governing our own lives. Our self-centered, selfish society knows very little about any other pronoun than "me," "mine," or "I." But when God invades a life through the kingdom of grace, this self-centered orientation should change and the preoccupation of our prayer should be the next petition, "Your will be done." How can we say that we are in Christ, and have embraced the Lordship of Christ and crowned Him as our Sovereign, if we have more concern for our own cause than His?

As kingdom citizens we must be aware of the spiritual warfare in which we are engaged. I encourage anyone to read *Precious Remedies Against Satan's Devices* (Banner of Truth Trust), written by a Puritan pastor, Thomas Brooks, in 1652. Brooks exposes the most common temptation strategies that the accuser of the brethren (Revelation 12:10) uses to damage the members of God's regiment. In our postmodern age, the need for a rallying call to the Church is paramount. Although this is the briefest of the petitions in the Disciples' Prayer, it is also the most far-reaching. In praying "Your Kingdom come" we plead for the power and blessing of the Holy Spirit to attend the preaching of the Word, and for the overthrow of Christ's enemies. We are praying for the destruction of Satan's domain. Thus, we pray that the kingdom of grace may be further extended till the whole of God's elect are brought into it. By implication we are praying that God will wean us more and more from the system of this world and its perishing attractions.

Consider some of the uses to which our "Battle Cry" can be applied. First, we ought to mourn and confess our own failures to promote the Kingdom of God. It is our duty to confess before God our wretched, natural depravity and the repetitious proclivity of our flesh to serve sin and the interests of Satan (Romans 7:14-24). We ought to mourn the sad state of the world and its hunger for political correctness, and the woeful transgressions of God's Law, by which God is dishonored and the kingdom of Satan furthered (Psalm 119:136; Mark 3:5). Second, we are to earnestly seek those graces that will make our lives a sanctifying influence in the world, that we may be "salt and light" in order that God's kingdom might be both revealed and maintained. We are to strive to subject ourselves to the commandments of Christ as a love response in obedience, always ready to do His bidding (Romans 6:13). Third, having prayed for God's enabling, we are to perform all the responsibilities assigned to us by God so that the fruits that pertain to God's kingdom will be evident (Matthew 21:43; Romans 14:17). This we are to do with all diligence (Ecclesiastes 9:10; Colossians 3:17), using all the divinely appointed means for the furthering of God's kingdom and the destruction of the enemy. Fourth, we must pray that our pulpits will be filled with men who will preach Christ and Him crucified and rally the remnant around our "Battle Cry."

May God bind our hearts in humble allegiance to the cross and render us more radiant for the benefit of a dark and perishing world, to the praise of the glory of His grace and the furtherance of his kingdom, praying, "YOUR KINGDOM COME."

Resources cited and for further study:

*The Lord's Prayer*, Arthur Pink

*Baker New Testament Commentary: Matthew,*
William Hendrickson

*The Sermon on the Mount,* D. A. Carson

*The Sermon on the Mount: An Expositional Commentary,*
James Montgomery Boice

*The Puritans on Prayer:* John Preston, Nathaniel Vincent,
Samuel Lee

*A Body of Divinity,* Thomas Watson

# Postscript

When our Lord taught on prayer, He did not tell us necessarily to "pray these words," but rather to "pray in this manner." The manner in which we pray is every bit as important as the words we use in prayer. This is what the venerable authors in this book have tried to address, the manner of our prayers.

R. C. Sproul told us that we pray because Christ has commanded it of us, and because it is one of the means by which God brings His will to pass.

John MacArthur reminded us that prayer is an act of worship, so our prayers should be worshipful, reverential, and worthy of God's majesty.

John Piper showed us that God is to be the focus of our prayer life, not ourselves and our circumstances. When Jesus taught on prayer, God's honor was first and foremost on His lips.

Joel Beeke explained what it is to hallow God's name. If this was the primary concern of our Lord, it should be our primary concern as well, especially in our prayer lives as much as in our daily lives. And to do this we must know God intimately.

Steven J. Lawson clarified for us that to pray "in Jesus' name" is not simply to attach a little catch phrase at the end of our prayer that will insure that we are heard, but to pray in confidence that what we pray for is the very same thing that our Lord would pray for. It is to pray consistent with the character and will of God.

Robert Godfrey said that prayer is not a place for us to get God to do our will, but rather a place for us to seek His will. And our prayers will show us how closely we are in tune with the will of God.

Richard Phillips showed us how prayer is consistent with the sovereignty of God. Rather than avoiding prayer due to an unbiblical fatalism, we actually pray more confidently *because* God is sovereign.

Hywel Jones explained that praying in Christ's name is something that only believers can do since His first coming. We now have a privilege that earlier believers did not have.

Michael Haykin expounded the importance of corporate prayer for the church. Not only are our individual prayers significant, but our prayers as a corporate body are also.

Phil Johnson made clear what the "effectual, fervent prayer of a righteous man" is, and what characterizes the prayers of such a man or woman—that it is private, passionate, and persistent.

And, lastly, Bruce Bickel showed us that prayer is like a war cry for the believer, a rallying cry, where we, as Christian soldiers, prepare for our spiritual battles by prayer.

May it please the Lord to use this book to encourage the hearts of His people to unite in prayer for His glory, for their holiness, and for the kingdom of God to flourish.

There is a study guide available for use with this book. Go to, www.northamptonpress.org to download the PDF file.)

# Other Titles from The Northampton Press

**Sermons on the Lord's Supper,** by Jonathan Edwards. Contains 15 sermons by the great New England preacher, 13 of which were previously unpublished. 272 pages HB

**Sermons on Important Doctrines,** by John Colquhoun. A great Scottish preachers deals with justification, sanctification, salvation from sin, Christ as our righteousness, and others. 252 pages HB.

**The Christian Father's Present to His Children,** by John Angell James. This book shows that the best gift any father can leave his children is a godly upbringing. 326 pages HB

**Heaven Taken by Storm,** by Thomas Watson. Watson shows the "holy violence" required to storm the gates of heaven. 148 pages HB

**Saving Faith,** by John Colquhoun. This book distinguishes true faith from its counterfeits. 300 pages HB

**Light and Heat: The Puritan View of the Pulpit,** by Dr. R. Bruce Bickel. The best book on Puritan preaching in print today. 180 pages HB

**Distinguishing Traits of Christian Character,** by Gardiner Spring. What marks a man as a true child of God? Which ones cannot be counterfeited? 150 pages, HB

**Studies on Saving Faith,** by Arthur Pink. This is a hard-hitting rebuttal to the "easy-believism" that is so prevalent in our day. It shows that repentance is necessary for salvation. 217 pages, HB

**A Dialogue Between a Catholic Priest and a Protestant,** by Matthew Poole. A debate over the issues dividing these two very different faiths. 145 pages, HB.

**The Precious Things of God,** by Octavius Winslow. A warm devotional book that lists those things that God finds precious. 280 pages, HB.

**Sighs From Hell,** by John Bunyan. The author of *Pilgrim's Progress* was also a fine Bible expositor. This is his treatment of Luke 16, a story Christ told of Dives and Lazarus. It is especially timely in light of a popular mega-church pastor's book denying a literal hell. 168 pages. HB

**Preparing For Eternity,** by Mike Gendron. The author was a devout Roman Catholic for 34 years before God opened his eyes to biblical and doctrinal truth. He compares Romanist dogma with Scripture truth. Topics such as the proper role of Mary, the ultimate source of authority, the mass, purgatory, the sufficiency of Christ's sacrifice, and others are examined. 250 pages. PB.

**Faith,** by Jeremiah Burroughs. This book is comprised of two extremely scarce titles by this beloved Puritan preacher: *Precious Faith* and *The Saints' Walk by Faith,* neither of which has been in print since the 17th century. 288 pages. HB